AF669820

IT'S A RICH MAN'S WORLD

Also by the Authors

Girls Just Wanna Have Funds
Girls Just Wanna Have Impact Funds

IT'S A RICH MAN'S WORLD

Why Money Is Broken for Women and How We Fix It

CAMILLA FALKENBERG, EMMA DUE BITZ
AND ANNA-SOPHIE HARTVIGSEN

ORION
IGNITE

First published in Great Britain in 2026 by Orion Ignite,
an imprint of The Orion Publishing Group Ltd
Carmelite House, 50 Victoria Embankment
London EC4Y 0DZ

An Hachette UK Company

The authorised representative in the EEA is Hachette Ireland, 8 Castlecourt Centre, Dublin 15, D15 XTP3, Ireland (email: info@hbgi.ie)

When reading this book, please keep in mind that it does not constitute financial, legal or medical advice. Please ensure that you take advice from qualified and regulated financial, legal and/or medical professionals and practitioners before making decisions or taking action that could affect either your financial or medical wellbeing or for your legal protection.

1 3 5 7 9 10 8 6 4 2

Copyright © Camilla Falkenberg, Emma Due Bitz and
Anna-Sophie Hartvigsen 2026.

The moral right of Camilla Falkenberg, Emma Due Bitz and
Anna-Sophie Hartvigsen to be identified as the authors
of this work has been asserted in accordance with the
Copyright, Designs and Patents Act of 1988.

Diagrams by dkbcreative (pp.17, 69, 85 and 123).

All rights reserved. No part of this publication may be
reproduced, stored in a retrieval system, or transmitted
in any form or by any means, electronic, mechanical,
photocopying, recording, or otherwise, without the
prior permission of both the copyright owner and the
above publisher of this book.

A CIP catalogue record for this book is
available from the British Library.

ISBN (Hardback) 978 1 3987 2564 5
ISBN (Export Trade Paperback) 978 1 3987 2565 2
ISBN (Ebook) 978 1 3987 2567 6
ISBN (Audio) 978 1 3987 2570 6

Typeset by Input Data Services Ltd, Bridgwater, Somerset
Printed in Great Britain by Clays Ltd, Elcograf S.p.A.

FSC www.fsc.org MIX Paper | Supporting responsible forestry FSC® C104740

www.orionbooks.co.uk

CONTENTS

INTRODUCTION

By Anna-Sophie, Camilla and Emma

We are living in a rich man's world.

When we started Female Invest in 2019, our mission was simple: we wanted to help women take control of their money. We were frustrated by the financial advice aimed at women. Too often, it focused on saving money by skipping cappuccinos or cutting back on clothes and beauty – advice that felt patronising and failed to take women's ambitions seriously. We believed that if women learnt not only how to budget, but also to invest and build real wealth, it would transform their lives. And in many ways, it did. We saw thousands of women across the world step into their financial power, start investing for the first time, and build confidence and a growth mindset they had been told wasn't for them.

But the deeper we went into this work, the clearer it became that something much bigger was at play. Women are falling behind financially in every country, not because they lack discipline or the desire to build wealth, but because the world itself was never designed with us in mind. From medicine to marriage, housing to healthcare, labour markets to legal systems, the structures shaping our lives are designed by men, for men, often without any consideration of women's needs, realities or rights. That design still defines the world we live in.

Money is power. And right now, men have most of it.

Globally, men own $105 trillion more wealth than women

– forty-one times the size of the UK economy. At the current rate of progress, it will take 123 years to close the financial gender gap.[1]

These numbers are almost too big to process. They sound abstract, like something that happens to 'other people'. But this isn't just an intangible statistic. It shows up in your life, every single day.

It's in your payslip, where the average woman earns less than the man sitting next to her doing the same job. It's in your pension, where women retire with 30% less,[2] leaving many without the freedom to choose how to spend their later years. It's in your shopping basket, where the so-called pink tax means you pay more for everyday products simply because they're marketed to women.[3] It's in the invisible hours of unpaid care work, worth $10.8 trillion a year, that women shoulder without recognition or reward.[4]

Financial inequality isn't only about salaries and investing. It's about opportunity, power, and the ability to make decisions over your own life. It shows up in the cost of motherhood, access to education, healthcare and safety. It shapes career progression, relationship choices and even how women age. The bill for being a woman is constant, and it's climbing.

The result? Women face higher costs, earn less, save less, invest less and end up with less wealth. Not because we aren't ambitious, or because we don't work hard enough. But because the system was never built for us to thrive financially.

That reality is suffocating. It means fewer choices: relationships we can't afford to leave, careers we can't risk and futures that feel prewritten. Meanwhile, the people who hold the money are the ones making the decisions about our economies, our healthcare, our climate and even our bodies.

This inequality didn't happen by accident. It happened by

design. The good news is that what has been designed can be redesigned. What has been built can be rebuilt. Every woman who learns to understand, navigate and use money to create freedom for themselves is part of that change.

Changing the script

From the moment we are born, we absorb messages about money – some subtle, some overt, all powerful. These are money scripts: the beliefs and stereotypes about wealth that shape how we think, feel and act with money. Girls are often socialised to be cautious, to save more, take fewer risks and to defer ambition. Pop culture reinforces this, from Carrie Bradshaw buying shoes she cannot afford to the countless stories that frame women as inherently frivolous or financially incapable. We grow up hearing phrases like 'girls aren't good with money' or the more recent meme-ified 'girl maths', and over time these scripts become reality. They influence the choices we make in our careers, the risks we take, the way we manage our finances, and our sense of self-worth. They are invisible barriers, woven into how we see ourselves and our possibilities.

This book is here to rewrite that script. To challenge the stereotypes we were taught, to expose the societal forces that reinforce them and to empower women to take control of their financial lives. Changing the story we tell ourselves about money is the first step to reclaiming the power, freedom and opportunity that has always been ours.

We are the founders of Female Invest, a company we built from scratch with one radical idea: to close the financial gender gap by educating women on money management. What began as a passion project quickly grew into a global movement with paying members in 130+ countries on our learning app. At the time of writing, we've raised $24 million in funding, breaking glass ceilings in finance and entrepreneurship. We've been recognised by *Forbes*, written multiple bestselling books, broken multiple world records and built a movement that has reached women from every corner of the world, including Hillary Clinton and Emma Watson. But if there's one thing we've learnt along the way, it's this: financial literacy alone isn't enough.

That's where this book comes in.

We didn't set out to write another how-to guide. We've already written that, it's called *Girls Just Wanna Have Funds*, and it's helped women around the world take control of their finances and start investing. Rather, this book is about seeing the world clearly and understanding the rules we've been taught to follow, the stereotypes we've absorbed since childhood, the social contracts we've been pressured into and the historical legacies that shape our choices before we even realise it.

We want you to read this book with curiosity, and with courage. We want you to question the things you've been told are 'normal' or 'just the way things are'. We want you to imagine new possibilities for your own life, whether that means leaving bad relationships, saying no unapologetically, or investing in yourself with the conviction that you deserve to build wealth and security. We hope that in the pages of this book, you will find actionable steps and ways to move forward in this world, and the power to do so.

How to read this book

Every chapter starts with a short summary and a few key facts to give you a basic understanding of the issues we will cover. Throughout the book, we've included personal anecdotes to draw parallels from our own lives in the hope that you'll recognise parts of your own journey in them too. Because by showing how these mechanisms play out in everyday life, it becomes easier to understand their impact – and to see how we might change them.

You'll also notice fact boxes, practical tips and tasks sprinkled throughout the book. These aren't random, they're designed to give you concrete tools and actionable steps to apply what you're learning.

You don't need to read the chapters in order, you can jump around as you wish. Think of this book as a toolkit: dip into the chapters that speak to you, return to them when you need strength, and use them as fuel to break free. As you move through the book, look for the links to your own story. Where have you been asked to shrink? Where have you carried more than your share?

These are not abstract ideas: they are mirrors. Some of these mirrors and truths will be uncomfortable or challenging. We decided not to shy away from the hard realities, because we believe that facing them is the first step towards necessary change.

The hours spent with this book in your hands are not just an investment in your knowledge. They are an investment in your power, your freedom and your future.

NAVIGATING INTERSECTIONALITY

When we talk about 'women', it's tempting to imagine a single, unified experience. But the reality is, there is no one way of being a woman. Women are not a homogenous group, and any honest conversation about gender inequality must recognise that some women face not just one barrier, but many.

This is where intersectionality comes in. Coined by legal

scholar Kimberlé Crenshaw in 1989, the term describes how different forms of discrimination – such as racism, sexism, classism, homophobia or ableism – intersect and overlap. It is not simply that women of colour, for example, face racism and sexism as separate issues. These forces combine in unique ways, creating compounded disadvantages. The same is true for women living with disabilities, queer women, immigrant women, and women whose socio-economic background limits their opportunities. Each identity interacts with gender, shaping lived experience in ways that cannot be separated.

This matters because in almost every area we explore in this book – wealth, work, relationships, health – women from marginalised groups are disproportionately disadvantaged. Wage gaps are larger. Access to capital is harder. Leadership opportunities are scarcer. Healthcare outcomes are worse. These inequities are not accidents of the present moment; they are deeply rooted in historical systems of slavery, colonisation, segregation and exclusion that continue to shape society today. To discuss gender without acknowledging these realities would be incomplete.

Throughout this book, we have made every effort to be inclusive, drawing on research and perspectives from around the world. At the same time, we want to be transparent about the scope of this book. Entire volumes could, and should, be written about each of these overlapping issues through an intersectional lens. In this book, we have chosen to focus primarily on gender as a framework. That decision was not easy, because it risks making invisible the very differences we want to honour. Focusing on gender as a through line allows us to keep a clear focus on the patterns and structures that affect women more broadly, while recognising that these patterns manifest differently across groups.

We also recognise that the distinction between sex and gender is complex, and that not all women, including trans women and non-binary people, will experience these challenges in the same way. This is particularly evident in areas such as health, where lived experiences can diverge significantly, and where there is still a lack of research and data that includes trans women. This means that, even though our approach is explicitly trans-inclusive, the data often does not include trans women. When we refer to 'women', we mean anyone who identifies as a woman, recognising that trans women face additional barriers and discrimination that intersect with gender.

Much of what we write is also shaped by our own perspective as women living in the Western world. The obstacles faced by women in other parts of the globe (whether due to laws, cultural expectations, political instability or access to basic rights) would make this book look very different if written from their vantage point.

So, while this book focuses primarily on gender, we invite you to keep intersectionality in mind as you read. It is the lens that reminds us that progress for women cannot mean progress only for some women. It is a reminder that the fight for equality must always be inclusive, because none of us are free until all of us are free.

And finally, to be clear: this book is not anti-men. It is, however, unapologetically critical of the systems that have historically and persistently held women back. We invite men to read this book too, not defensively, but with curiosity. Our challenge to these systems comes from a place of hope and expectation. We want more, better and fairer for everyone – and that includes calling on men to rise alongside us, to engage, to question and to do better.

So let's begin.

MARRIED MEN ARE THE REAL GOLD-DIGGERS

By Camilla

There's one financial truth we never hear said out loud: the real 'gold-diggers' aren't the women who marry rich – they're the men who expect their wife to clean the house, raise the kids, work full time, carry the mental load, and still split the bills 50/50.

FACT SHEET

- On average, women in the UK spend twice as much time doing housework as men, even if they are in work and their partners are unemployed.[1]
- 70% of divorce filings are made by women.[2]
- 56% of married women hand over financial decisions to their husbands.
- 80% of women end up single (and the majority get negative financial surprises).
- Men are six times more likely than women to leave their spouse if she gets a life-altering health condition.[3]

For most of my twenties, I felt a quiet panic ticking in the background of everything I did. Not about my career or my goals, but about time and whether I was running out of it. I never questioned why I felt that way. I just assumed I had to find a partner and settle down. That there was a timeline, and I was behind. The idea of being single in my thirties felt like something to avoid at all costs. It wasn't until much later that I asked myself the most obvious question of all: what did I even need a partner for? And did I *actually* want children? I had never stopped to consider it. I had internalised the pressure so deeply, I forgot to ask whether the destination I was racing towards was one I even wanted.

I look back and I feel a huge amount of compassion for that version of myself. From the time we're little girls, the message is clear: a woman's happy ending begins with a wedding. From the fairy tales our parents read us to the Christmas movies where the big-city career girl settles down in a small countryside town, the narrative is always the same: love is the goal, and marriage is the reward. You can be smart, ambitious, even rebellious . . . but only in the aim of helping you fall in love and 'settle down'. Then the story ends. Happily, of course.

It's subtle, but powerful. Over time, it does something dangerous: it teaches us that no matter what we accomplish, it won't matter unless we have a ring on our finger and a man on our arm. That marriage is not just an option, but the ultimate proof of our worth.

But as I grew up, I watched those fairy-tale endings play out in real life. I watched women who followed the traditional path – marriage, children, the whole script, checking every box – and still felt empty. I saw how often it came at the cost of their own ambition. How they gave up careers they once loved, put their aspirations on hold, and slowly let go of the parts of themselves that didn't fit the role they were expected to play. Self-sacrifice became the standard, and fulfilment was something they kept postponing, hoping it might come later, once everyone else's needs were met.

The older I got, the more my aspirations seemed to clash with societal expectations. I wanted freedom. I wanted purpose. I wanted to live on my own terms. Yet deep down, I was still chasing a dream that had been planted in me before I was old enough to question it.

This dilemma is financial too.

At Female Invest, we talk a lot about long-term thinking, smart planning and financial independence. But there's one decision that quietly shapes all the others, which we rarely discuss. Spoiler alert: it's not your salary, not your portfolio, not your mortgage.

It's your partner.

And not only whether they earn well, invest or save responsibly, but whether they support your ambitions without flinching. Whether they assume your career will bend around theirs. Whether they show up when things get hard or quietly opt out when the emotional labour gets inconvenient.

With the right partner, romantic relationships can be amazing and elevate every area of your life. But when a big imbalance creeps in, the effects aren't only emotional. They're financial, too. And the numbers are sobering.

Very few of us are encouraged to treat our choice of life partner like the financial decision it is – to ask hard questions, look past chemistry, and plan not only for love but for equity. And we should. The wrong partner might not sabotage you outright, but they'll slowly chip away at your energy, your clarity, your upward momentum. The way compound interest works, but in reverse.

I've watched it unfold in the lives of brilliant, ambitious women – women who gradually shrink to fit relationships that were too small for their aspirations. I know this not just because I've seen it. I know it because I've lived it.

This chapter isn't here to discourage relationships or to suggest you should prioritise your career over everything else if that's not your path. We all need long-term human connection, in whatever form that takes. So our aim with this chapter is to open your eyes to the financial impact your choice of partner can have, regardless of your gender, orientation, or relationship style – and to help you navigate the tricky decisions and conversations that come with it.

THE ORIGIN OF MARRIAGE

Marriage can be wonderful. With the right person, it has potential to improve every part of your life, from your happiness and health to your finances. Sadly, the opposite is also often true, and statistically speaking married women are unhappier than single women.[4]

For centuries, marriage was not just a personal decision, it was a legal contract that stripped women of their financial independence. Under English common law, a married woman's legal identity was effectively erased in a doctrine known as *coverture*.

This meant that her husband took ownership of her property, her wages and her dowry. She could not sign contracts, own land or control her income. Even her personal belongings were legally considered her husband's property.[5] The system effectively made women financially dependent, with marriage acting less as a partnership and more as a legal transfer of wealth and power between men.

This wasn't unique to England. In France, the Napoleonic Code of 1804 made women legally subordinate to their husbands, stating explicitly that 'a wife owes obedience to her husband'.[6] Women needed their husband's permission to work, open a bank account or travel. In West Germany, married women could not work without their husband's permission until 1977.[7] And in the United States, it wasn't until 1974 that married women could open a bank account without their husband's consent.[8] These are just a few examples, and various forms of these laws were seen across the globe.

In many parts of the world today, echoes of these laws still exist. In Saudi Arabia, women needed male permission to obtain a passport and travel until 2019. And according to the UN, twenty countries still allow rapists to marry their victims to escape criminal prosecution.[9,10]

This global history has real consequences. It's why, even today, women across cultures are more likely to give up financial independence in marriage, whether through career sacrifices, unpaid domestic labour or an unequal division of financial decision-making.

The historical idea that marriage 'protects' women has long masked the reality: that for most of history, it financially disempowered them.

It wasn't until women began organising and resisting in the 19th century that things slowly began to change,[11] from the suffragettes demanding property rights alongside voting rights to married women challenging their legal status in court. This fight was never just about freedom, it was about access to capital, control and survival.

In many ways, that fight is still not over.

Looking at these facts, the branding of marriage as the ultimate dream for girls seems like the scam of the century. Historically, the concept of marriage was never about romance or love: it was a tool to control women.

MARRIAGE TODAY

Taking it easy has never been my strong suit. I have big dreams and visions for the future. My head is usually full of tasks, urgency and impatience. I love to learn new things, work long hours, and get lost in topics that interest me . . . sometimes too much. While I like to think that my personality keeps life exciting, I've also learnt it can be intense and hard to keep up with.

In relationships, that energy hasn't always been easy to hold. My past partners were kind people, supportive in their own ways, but some of them preferred stability, simplicity and traditional gender roles. There was an unspoken assumption that their careers would take priority, and that if we had children, I would naturally be the one to step back. That's the script many of us – men and women – are still handed, whether we realise it or not.

Had those relationships worked out, I think I would've lost more than momentum. I would've lost the version of myself that moves towards ideas without hesitation, the part that doesn't apologise for wanting more.

It's such a paradox. For most people (myself included), the idea of marriage is about having a partner to go through life with. Someone who will support you and share the burdens of life with you . . . Right?

While this dream of partnership is often sold in modern-day marriage, it's not what reality looks like for most married couples. Because in practice, rather than offloading responsibilities when partnering, women who marry men tend to gain tasks and domestic work, resulting in less time to pursue their careers, hobbies or even health. In 1989, sociologists Arlie Hochschild and Anne Machung coined the term 'second shift' to describe the unpaid work women do at home after finishing their paid job.[12] More than thirty years later, the term is still painfully accurate.

Is an extraordinary man just an average woman?

The unpaid labour of women – particularly married women – is the invisible engine that keeps our economy and society running. Research conducted by the Pew Research Center shows that married women *still* do the majority of unpaid labour, even when they are the main breadwinner. Of course, these numbers show *averages*, and we know that there are also amazing, equal male partners out there.

But looking at the average workload distribution: if American women were paid just minimum wage for their unpaid work at home and in caregiving roles, they would earn around $1.5 trillion per year.[13] Globally, the number climbs to $10.8 trillion annually – comparable to the size of the entire tech industry, and roughly 9% of the world's entire GDP.[14] That's the scale of work that goes unrecognised and uncompensated.

Caregiving and household work: an unequal balance between parents

Men spend less time per week on caregiving and household work, even when they earn an income equal to their wives'

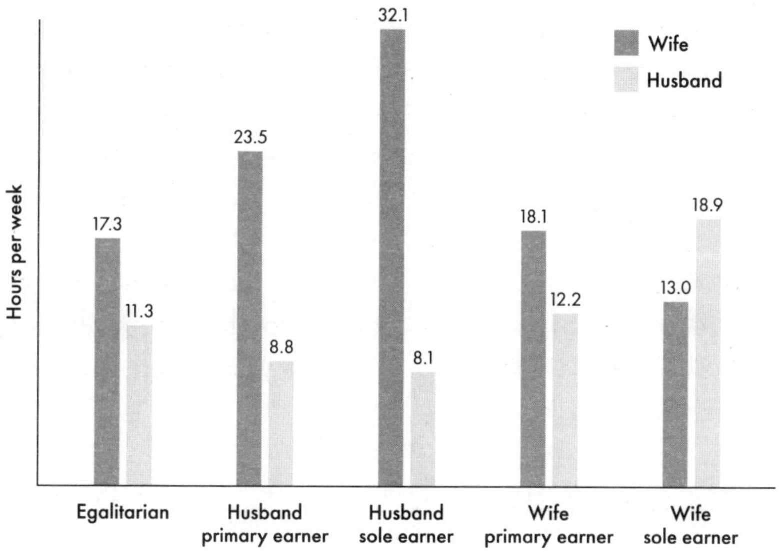

Source: 'In a Growing Share of U.S. Marriages, Husbands and Wives Earn About the Same.' Pew Research Center (2015).[15]

The married men who benefit from this labour wouldn't be able to do the same amount of paid work outside the home, to the same standard, if they didn't have someone to cook their food, clean their home, wash their clothes, raise their children and manage the mental load that keeps the household running. Imagine what women could achieve if we too had a wife at home, supporting every aspect of our life. In heterosexual households, it's this invisible labour that enables one partner to thrive professionally and increase their earning potential, while the other holds everything else together, unpaid.

Yet, we still refer to women who stay home as if they're 'not working'. Women have always worked. For generations, they've shouldered the burden of emotional, domestic and caregiving labour around the clock, while their husband's workday would end when he walked through the door. Even today, studies show that while men's labour tends to stop when they leave the (proverbial) office, women's continues: at home, after hours and often without acknowledgement.

Which makes you wonder: who's really benefiting here? If a man relies on his partner to manage the home and raise his children, then he's not a partner. He's a dependant.

Now, imagine how far women would go if the average husband offered the same level of support as the average wife. If a man did all of this on top of his career while also being emotionally available, he'd be called extraordinary – yet for many women, it's just expected. Maybe there's truth to the saying that an extraordinary man is really just an average woman.

Traditional gender roles also still impact how couples make financial decisions. A UBS study found that 56% of married women hand over financial decisions to their husbands.[16] That might seem like a personal preference, but it has real consequences, especially considering that 80% of women die single (due to widowhood or divorce).[17] Most of them will get negative financial surprises, not because they didn't contribute, but because they weren't involved in managing the money.[18]

The bigger picture is clear: marriage, as it exists today, often adds unpaid responsibilities to women's lives while making husbands' lives easier. These aren't isolated choices – they're patterns rooted in centuries of expectation.

We've spent too long calling women gold-diggers. Because when you look at the numbers, it might just be the other way around.

The lesbian wage premium

You might be wondering how this all plays out in same-sex relationships. The research is limited, but what we do know is interesting. According to Robert-Jay Green, who has studied LGBTQ+ relationships for decades, same-sex couples tend to be far more equal in how they handle things like decision-making, finances, housework and childcare. As he put it: 'Basically every dimension we looked at, same-sex couples are dramatically more equal in the way they function together as a couple compared to heterosexual couples.'[19] As a result, women in same-sex relationships tend to make more money and do significantly better financially.

According to the World Economic Forum, women in same-sex relationships make 9% more money on average. This phenomenon is also known as *the lesbian wage premium*.[20] This might be because women in same-sex relationships tend to share the burden of unpaid labour more equally, whereas women in heterosexual relationships tend to carry the vast majority of this burden.[21]

WHAT TRUE PARTNERSHIP MEANS

Although it might sound like it, this is not one long argument against marriage or building a life with someone you love. Quite the opposite.

While the risks of misalignment are real, the upside of true partnership – the kind built on mutual respect and shared ambition – is profound. When you find someone who meets you as an equal, the return on investment compounds. You move through life with a co-architect. A teammate. Someone who doesn't make your ambition feel like a burden or something to be ashamed of. Your energy stretches further. Your success becomes shared. And yes – you show up stronger. At work, in your relationship and, if you choose it, in motherhood.

That doesn't mean everything will be evenly split. Nor should it be. Expecting a perfect 50/50 balance at all times is not only unrealistic – it can quietly set you up for resentment.

One of my favourite authors, Brené Brown, once said something that stuck with me. In an interview, she called the idea of a constant 50/50 marriage 'the biggest crock of bullshit' she's ever heard. She's right. Real relationships don't run on rigid equity, they run on empathy. Brown and her husband have a simple but brilliant check-in: they regularly ask each other what percentage they're running at. If one says, 'I've only got 20% today', the other knows they need to bring 80. On days when they're both depleted, they shift into protection mode – prioritising kindness, softness and grace. It's not about who's doing more. It's about making sure neither of you falls through the cracks.

At the end of the day, your romantic partner won't just influence your happiness. They'll shape your entire future. That's why I'll say it one more time: your partner is the single most important financial decision you'll ever make.

And they're more than that. The right partnership, the kind that expands you rather than shrinks you, is worth holding out for.

So how do you know who's worth building a future with?

According to Logan Ury, author of *How to Not Die Alone*, we often choose partners based on chemistry or surface-level compatibility, rather than long-term alignment or emotional maturity. She calls it 'dating for a resumé' rather than 'dating for a life partner'.

What actually predicts long-term satisfaction, according to the research, isn't a perfectly curated checklist. It's whether someone is kind, emotionally stable and willing to grow with you. It's less about sparks and more about shared effort and teamwork. You're not choosing someone to go on a first date with. You're choosing someone to go through career changes, mortgage stress, parenting challenges and ageing with. Someone who will evolve with you, not hold you back.

Which brings us back to money. While love may be blind, money is not. No matter how stable or emotionally fulfilling your relationship is, the financial side needs its own attention. It might not be romantic, but it's certainly real, and ignoring it comes at a cost.

Be critical before you commit to someone, and make sure to discuss the basics:

- Do you want the same kind of lifestyle?
- Do your ambitions align?
- How do you handle money?
- At what age would you like to retire?
- Do you split responsibilities fairly?

Ask follow-up questions. Observe the answers. What are you willing to compromise on and what are you not?

HOW TO MANAGE YOUR FINANCES AS A COUPLE

Ask anyone in a long-term relationship what they fight about the most, and money is almost always at the top of the list. Within that? The question of *how* to manage your finances together.

Should you split things 50/50? Combine everything into one pot? Keep things completely separate? There's no one-size-fits-all answer, but this decision will shape your day-to-day dynamic and long-term power balance, so it's worth exploring all options and getting it right.

Times are changing. In the past, couples often merged everything by default: one bank account, one budget, one 'head of household' (usually the man). Today, with more women working, earning and making their own financial choices, that model doesn't automatically make sense for every couple.

What you choose isn't just about logistics. It's about values, fairness, independence, trust, and how you see the future. Let's break it down.

Option 1: Splitting your finances

This usually means each partner keeps their income, savings and debts separate, and you divide joint expenses (like rent, bills, groceries) in some way, often 50/50 or proportionally based on income.

Pros

- **Financial independence.** You don't have to justify your spending or feel like you need permission to buy something.
- **Privacy.** If you prefer to keep your finances to yourself (especially early in the relationship), this allows for boundaries.
- **Freedom for different habits.** One of you might love spreadsheets. The other might hate budgeting. Splitting means you don't need to align every detail.

Cons

- **Not all lifestyles are created equal.** A strict 50/50 split can lead to resentment if one person earns significantly less but still pays half. That means one person has a tighter lifestyle (smaller flat, fewer holidays, no cushion) while the other thrives.
- **It ignores unpaid labour.** If one partner takes on more domestic work (cleaning, cooking, childcare) but still pays half, the load is far from equal.
- **Emotional distance.** Keeping finances fully separate can signal a lack of shared commitment or long-term planning.

Key questions to ask

- Are we okay with differences in lifestyle based on income?
- How do we value non-financial contributions (like emotional or domestic labour)?
- Will we feel like true partners if our financial lives stay separate?

Option 2: Merging your finances

This means pooling your money (either all of it or most of it) into joint accounts and managing expenses, savings and planning as a team.

Pros

- **Shared goals, shared resources.** You're building a life together not just emotionally but financially too.

- **Redresses power imbalances.** If one partner earns less or takes time off for caregiving, merging ensures both have equal access and financial security.
- **Simplifies life.** One budget. One system. No need to manually transfer to each other for the electricity bill every month.

Cons

- **You take on each other's financial baggage.** If your partner has debt or bad credit, it can affect your shared goals and plans.
- **Harder to leave.** In the event of a break-up, disentangling your money (and emotions) can be legally and mentally messy.
- **'What's yours is mine' isn't always fair.** What happens if one of you entered the relationship with significantly more wealth or assets?

Key questions to ask

- Are we comfortable with full transparency, including past debts or bad habits?
- What safeguards do we want if the relationship ends?
- How do we handle inherited money or assets from before the relationship?

So what's the best option?

There isn't one. The healthiest couples are the ones who *consciously* choose a financial model that works for them, not the ones who fall into a pattern out of habit or pressure.

Some couples go fully merged. Others keep things separate but have a shared pot for joint expenses. Some revisit the arrangement as their relationship (and income levels) change. There's no gold star for doing it a certain way, but there is risk in not talking about it at all.

The best financial set-up is one that:

- Reflects your values
- Feels fair (not necessarily equal)
- Gives both partners agency and security
- Evolves over time.

Don't rush the decision. And definitely don't avoid it. The goal isn't just to pay bills, it's to build a life you both believe in.

WHAT ABOUT A PRENUP?

You've probably heard of prenups and wondered if you need one. The short answer? Yes.

A prenuptial agreement (or prenup) is simply a legal document you and your partner sign before marriage that outlines how your finances will be handled if the relationship ends. Think of it as an insurance policy: you hope you'll never need it, but if you do, you'll be glad it's there.

Here's the thing most people don't realise: even if you don't write your own prenup, you already have one. It's called *the law.* Every country has default rules about what happens to your money, assets and debts when a marriage ends. The question isn't whether you want a prenup, it's whether you want to choose your own rules or let the government decide for you.

And no, a prenup is not about ripping your partner off or

assuming your marriage will fail. It's about clarity. It's about sitting down, while you're both in love and on the same team, and figuring out what feels fair. Do you want to protect a business you built before marriage? Make sure debts aren't shared equally? Ensure that one partner isn't left financially stranded after years of unpaid care work? A prenup is the space to have those conversations openly, without bitterness or blame.

Far from being 'unromantic', a prenup is an act of love and respect. It says: *I value us enough to make sure we're protected no matter what happens.* And trust me, it's a lot easier to agree on what's fair when you're sharing a bottle of wine on a Saturday night than when you're fighting with lawyers years down the line.

So yes, you need a prenup. Not because you don't believe in your relationship, but because you believe in yourself. If you're already married, you can still make this agreement. It's then called a 'postnuptial agreement' (postnup), but it's exactly the same thing.

Quick Guide: How to get a prenup

1. **Start the conversation early**
   Bring it up before wedding planning takes over. Frame it as protecting *both* of you, not just yourself.
2. **List your assets and debts**
   Be transparent: savings, property, businesses, student loans, credit cards. Everything goes on the table.
3. **Decide what you want to protect**
   Think about: property you owned before marriage, inheritances, businesses, family money or future earnings.
4. **Talk about fairness**
   If one partner will pause their career for kids or take on

more unpaid work, discuss how that will be recognised financially.

5. **Hire lawyers (yes, both of you)**
   You'll each need independent legal advice to make the prenup valid. Even though it costs money, it's nothing compared to the cost of going through divorce without the right paperwork in place first.
6. **Sign it well before the wedding**
   Last-minute prenups can get challenged later. Aim to finalise it months in advance.

Pro tip: A prenup isn't set in stone forever. You can revisit it with a *postnup* if your circumstances change (for example, kids, career breaks, health problems, new businesses or unexpected wealth).

UNTIL DEATH (OR INCONVENIENCE) DO US PART

Talking about money early and often is not just about planning for the future you hope for. It's also about planning for the worst. Because even though no one gets married with the intention of breaking up, 50% of marriages do end in divorce.

To be clear: That's actually a great thing.

Not because we want marriages to fail, but because it's an expression of women having choice. As you might remember, women in the US weren't allowed to open a bank account until 1974. In the UK, women weren't even taxed independently until 1990, meaning that their income until that point was regarded as an addition to their husband's earnings. This effectively means that, until very recently, women were financially trapped in their marriage. Low divorce rates 'back in the day' didn't mean that couples were happier, it just meant that women weren't able to leave.

As I wrote at the beginning of this chapter, married women are consistently the unhappiest subgroup in the population. They are expected to do the majority of housework, the majority of childcare, emotional labour and mental load associated with running a family, often while juggling a full-time career. It should come as no surprise that 70% of divorce filings are made by women.[22] It's tempting to feel sad about the high divorce rates, but really they are an expression of women's financial liberation.

With that said, when a marriage ends, women are far more likely than men to suffer the financial consequences. While we often hear of a woman 'rinsing her ex-husband for everything he's worth', on average women experience a 41% drop in income after divorce, nearly double the average decrease men face. That gap isn't just a statistic, it's a reflection of systemic disadvantages that compound over time: the persistent wage gap, more frequent career breaks to care for children or family members, the lack of involvement in financial planning and the unequal burden of unpaid domestic work.

Pension gaps also widen dramatically after divorce. In many countries, retirement systems still aren't built to recognise unpaid caregiving work or the joint nature of long-term financial planning in marriage. In the UK, divorced women retire with 75% fewer savings compared to divorced men, according to Pensions Age.[23] These factors leave women with less earning power, fewer savings and more to lose.

For mothers, the challenges intensify. Around 80% of custodial parents are women, but fewer than half receive the full child support they're owed.[24] Even when payments do arrive, they rarely cover the true cost of raising children. This limits women's ability to work full time, save or invest in their futures.

As a result, rebuilding after divorce is a steeper climb for women, especially for those aged over fifty, who face a poverty rate of nearly 27%, almost double that of their male counterparts.

In short, divorce can shatter not just relationships but financial stability, and for women the fallout is far more severe. With that knowledge, it's even more astounding how many women choose poverty over staying with the wrong partner. What does that say about the quality of many heterosexual marriages?

When the grief is financial too

And for those who don't divorce? The story, sadly, doesn't always end more gently.

Half of women over the age of seventy-five are widowed.[25,26] For many women, widowhood doesn't just hollow out their life emotionally, it drains them financially too. Roughly 80% of women die single and that means most *will* manage their finances alone at some point. When most of them didn't participate in financial planning while their spouse was still alive, this can create a difficult situation to say the least.

Within the first two years of widowhood, women's income drops by 22%, and their wealth dips by 10%. While men's finances tend to stay stable after a spouse dies, women's savings keep dwindling, drawn down to cover everyday expenses.

Why? Women live longer, earn less, and often spend decades doing unpaid caregiving. That leaves them with lower retirement savings, smaller pensions and less social security. More than half of widowed women live pay cheque to pay cheque or struggle to cover basic bills. Nearly 40% carry significant debt, sometimes over $100,000. The financial strain lingers – into retirement, into ageing, into the years that were supposed to feel secure.

THE RUSH TO CHOOSE (AND WHY IT COSTS US)

Despite everything covered in this chapter, we raise young girls with the idea that getting married is the ultimate achievement. The messaging is consistent in all the communication they get growing up. As a result, many girls think they have a deadline, and that makes them more likely to settle for partners that aren't ideal.

As women, we're raised on timelines: marriage by thirty, children shortly after, a tidy home life to match. The message is clear, even if it's rarely said outright: don't wait too long, don't be too picky, and definitely don't expect too much. Layer on the biological clock, a real, unyielding presence for many women who want and can have children, and the pressure tightens. So we choose. Often quickly. Too often, we choose someone who seems 'good enough', without asking the harder questions about who they'll be not just in love, but in life.

Will they back your career the way you back theirs? Will they celebrate your ambition or wince when you succeed? Will they assume their professional path is non-negotiable while yours is flexible by default?

If you're a woman who wants a career and a family, or even just one of the two, and you find yourself – like so many do – in a relationship where the domestic and emotional labour disproportionately falls on you, that imbalance doesn't just stay at home. It shows up in your work. Your pay. Your future.

You can't scale in your career while working a second, invisible shift. And yet, many women do. Quietly. Sometimes resentfully.

Looking at all this data, it's easy to argue that modern-day marriage is still centred around the concept of women providing unpaid physical and emotional support to their spouse. While this line of thought may offend some people, it's backed by data as well: when women get seriously ill, they're far more likely to be left by their partners than the other way around. A study by the US National Institutes of Health found that women with life-altering health conditions are six times more likely to be abandoned by their male partners than men are by their female partners.[27] Why? For too many men, the emotional labour, caregiving and household responsibilities their wives have always handled suddenly fall on their shoulders, and they walk away instead of stepping up. It exposes a deep imbalance in how many heterosexual relationships are structured, where women are expected to nurture, support and sacrifice, but can't count on the same in return. Illness doesn't just make women physically vulnerable, it also reveals the fragility of the support systems they thought they had. In a culture that still socialises women to serve and men to receive, sickness becomes a breaking point. Not because the love dies, but because the service stops.[28]

THIS IS NOT AN ANTI-MARRIAGE ARGUMENT, IT'S A PRO-CHOICE ONE

While reading this, I wonder how many of you assumed that I am single and always have been. I can already hear the push-back coming: happily married women (and men) ready to argue that *their* marriage is nothing like what I'm describing.

Here's the thing: I'm not single. I'm in a happy, long-term relationship.

You can be in a happy relationship and *still* acknowledge that, for the majority of women, heterosexual marriage comes at a steep cost, negatively impacting their finances, happiness and health.

That's not a personal opinion. It's a documented pattern. Yet, every time we share these kinds of facts at Female Invest's social media, the comment section fills with people saying, 'Well, that's not true for me!'

That is amazing. Congratulations. But please remove your fingers from the keyboard, because your individual experience does not cancel out the overall trend.

We need to stop confusing individual stories with the bigger picture. Just because something isn't true for one person doesn't mean it's not a problem for *millions* of others. By dismissing real data with a single experience, we often make it much harder to have a proper discussion about a topic that's hard enough to discuss as it is.

And let me be clear: I'm not against marriage, relationships or love. I'm pro-choice – in every sense of the word. Every woman should be free to decide what kind of life, partnership or family she wants, without shame and without invisible financial traps waiting around the corner.

My goal isn't to scare you away from relationships, but rather to give you the tools to step into them with open eyes, clear boundaries and financial independence intact. When women know the risks and take steps to protect themselves, their relationships can become what they were always meant to be: a source of joy, connection and growth. Not a financial liability.

That's where the real hope lies. The more we normalise these conversations, the more freedom we create for all of us to build relationships that are rooted in equality, respect and love on our own terms.

HEALTH IS WEALTH

By Anna-Sophie

Our health shapes our lives: from our capacity to work and earn to the energy we bring to relationships, hobbies and personal growth. For women, it often comes at a steep cost. We live longer than men, yet those extra years are too often spent sick, navigating medical bills, lost income and opportunities that slip away unnoticed. Health isn't just personal – it's political, economic and life-defining.

FACT SHEET

- Women spend roughly 25% more of their lives in poor health compared to men.[1]
- On average, women are diagnosed four years later than men for the same diseases.[2]
- Only 1% of global health funding goes to research and innovation in female-specific conditions beyond cancer.[3]
- 70% of people living with chronic pain are women, yet 80% of the studies available on chronic pain were conducted on men or male animals.[4]
- Women in the UK spend approximately 50% more on out-of-pocket healthcare expenses than men.[5]
- Reproductive health conditions cost the UK economy £11 billion every year due to lost working days.[6]
- Closing the women's health gap could unlock over $1 trillion in global GDP by 2040.[7]
- For every $1 invested in women's health, the economy would gain at least $3.[8]

It was December 2020, and the past few weeks had been extraordinarily stressful – the kind of stress that settles in your chest and doesn't leave. Over the summer, after months of pitching, we had finally secured a group of incredible investors for Female Invest's first funding round. We'd agreed on the valuation and the investment amount. Everything seemed locked in. We were convinced the money would land any day, and we were under time pressure to meet our targets, so we got to work. We started hiring, investing in growth, rebuilding our website and improving our product. We had a plan. What we didn't have – at least, not yet – was the money.

As first-time founders, we didn't realise how long the legal process of receiving the funding would be. We thought the hard part was over once the due diligence was completed and the investors said yes. Naively, we assumed that the logistics would be smooth and quick. But the paperwork dragged on, and we learnt the hard way that it's normal for the legal process to take weeks. And because we were so inexperienced, it took even longer.

Meanwhile, the bills started stacking up. Rent, salaries, suppliers – all payments that we had scheduled to go out before the investment landed. By the time we reached December, the numbers were clear: if the money didn't arrive soon, we'd be bankrupt by January. It was an incredibly stressful time. We were working around the clock, operating on hope, faith and fumes.

One morning, in the middle of all of this, I woke up to the sound of my alarm. I stretched, blinked a few times, and reached for my phone. But something was wrong: my vision was so blurry I could barely make out the screen. I tried rubbing my eyes, but the burning only intensified. I was living alone at the time and had no one to turn to. Panicked, I tapped out my dad's number – one of the few I knew by muscle memory.

He picked up, and I told him I thought I had an eye infection. He'd had them before when I was growing up, and I trusted he'd know what to do. He asked me to go to the bathroom and check if my eyes were red. I stumbled across the apartment, turned on the light and stood in front of the mirror. But I couldn't tell if my eyes were red. I couldn't even make out the shape of my face. My nose blurred into my mouth, my eyes into shadows. That's when fear started setting in.

I tried to google an eye doctor, but I could barely read the letters on my screen despite zooming in to the max. After endless fumbling and failed attempts, I finally found a clinic that could see me four hours later. Those four hours felt like forever. I lay in a foetal position in bed, eyes burning, vision fading, pain growing with every minute.

When I finally made it to the clinic, the doctor examined me and delivered the diagnosis: a severe case of uveitis in both eyes. Uveitis is an autoimmune disease where your immune system attacks your eyes. If left untreated (or if treatment fails) it can lead to blindness, an outcome that is not uncommon. In fact, uveitis is a leading cause of blindness in the developed world.[9]

I was sent home with a steroid-based treatment and a chilling warning: 'Because of the high dose you'll need, there's a 50% chance this medication will cause cataracts, which makes you go blind. But at least that type of blindness is operable, the blindness from uveitis is not.'

I don't think I fully understood the gravity of those words.

Over the following week, the medication didn't work. I lost my vision completely. Days blurred together in darkness. I couldn't read, couldn't walk outside, couldn't eat without fumbling for food. Even the smallest things – brushing my teeth, finding the toilet – felt unmanageable. It's needless to say that doing any type of work was impossible – and with everything going on with the business, the timing couldn't have been worse.

At my next appointment, the doctor took one look at me and said, 'I'm afraid to touch your eyes.' He referred me immediately to the emergency room of the country's best eye hospital, where I was admitted for intensive treatment. I spent the next two months living in uncertainty, in and out of hospitals, fighting for my vision.

I'm relieved to say that, as spring arrived, my vision gradually returned to normal. By then, the funding round had closed, but the impact of my time away was undeniable – the business had taken a hit, and it took months to fully recover.

This was not a happy ending.

Like all autoimmune diseases, uveitis doesn't just disappear. It hides, waits, flares up, especially under stress. It has been back since, and each time it appears, I'm consumed by the fear that this time the blindness will be permanent. Even now, as I write this, I can feel that same heaviness return. My stomach tightens and my hands tremble. Not from memory alone, but from the fear that it could (and most likely will) happen again.

Last year another one of us developed acute IBS, a disease that causes weeks-long flare-ups with extreme stomach pain, bloating and diarrhoea. It's a terrible syndrome that, similar to my uveitis, is chronic and triggered by stress and anxiety. Now imagine dealing with that in the middle of investor meetings, on long flights, or on stage at major events.

We're not alone. In fact, 80% of autoimmune disease patients are women.

Someone once told me *you don't have a problem until you have a health problem*, and that has lived rent-free in my head ever since. We've experienced first-hand how devastating the consequences of poor health can be on all aspects of our life, including our career and finances.

Health and money are inseparable, and women are facing a unique set of challenges. Without good health, the ability to make and manage money can be significantly impacted, whether it's taking time off work, struggling with focus due to chronic pain or dealing with the mental load of navigating the healthcare system.

At the same time, health issues also often come with a price tag. From therapy sessions to prescriptions to private care when public systems fall short (or, indeed, are non-existent), staying healthy isn't always an affordable solution.

This chapter is here to connect the dots. To show how deeply health affects your financial life, and the unique challenges that women face in this regard. We also want to show that protecting your well-being is not only a question of self-care. It's a financial decision. Because without health, there is no wealth.

WOMEN LIVE LONGER BUT SPEND MORE YEARS SICK

You've heard it before: 'Women live longer than men.' But here's the part no one talks about. Women spend a larger part of their lives in poor health. In fact, women live an average of five years longer than men, but they spend eight more years in poor health. That means women may be living longer, but they're also living sicker.[10]

This is also known as the gender health gap, and it shows up in nearly every health statistic we have across the world. According to the World Health Organization, women spend roughly 25% more of their lives in poor health.[11] For example, women are more likely than men to suffer from autoimmune diseases and chronic illnesses, are more likely to live with pain, and twice as likely to suffer from depression and anxiety. Conditions like migraines, long-term fatigue, reproductive health issues and hormone-related complications also disproportionately affect women, and yet they are often under-researched and under-treated.[12–16] While many of these conditions aren't fatal, they are debilitating, requiring constant management, extended time off work, specialist appointments and ongoing medication. Not to mention menopause, which has such a significant and widespread impact on women's financial lives that we've included a whole chapter on it later in this book.

The fact that women get sick more often is made worse by the fact that women are also dismissed more often when seeking professional help. Across every part of the healthcare system, studies show that women are taken less seriously when seeking help. In many cases, this has dangerous consequences.[17] When it comes to pain, women wait longer in emergency rooms and are less likely to receive proper treatment. One study found that women who arrived at the emergency room with chest pain waited 29% longer than men to be evaluated for a possible heart attack.[18] And when women are (finally) evaluated, they are more likely to be dismissed. For example, middle-aged women complaining of chest pain are twice as likely to be diagnosed with a mental health disorder compared to male counterparts who exhibit the exact same symptoms.[19]

This kind of dismissal shows up in the treatment of reproductive issues, chronic illnesses and everyday physical pain. There are so many studies we could cite here, all showing the same trend: doctors are more likely to assume women are exaggerating their symptoms or being overly emotional compared to men.[20]

A concrete consequence of this is that women are diagnosed later than men. A large Danish study found that women are diagnosed an average of four years later compared to men across 770 diseases including cancer, diabetes and cardiovascular conditions.[21]

The result is a painful paradox. Women get sick more often, but are taken less seriously when they do. They are forced to become their own advocates, repeatedly pushing for answers in a system that was not built for them.

If you add race into the conversation, these statistics become even more shocking. Race plays a major role in how patients are seen, heard and treated. In particular, Black women sit at one of the most dangerous intersections of healthcare discrimination. Across nearly every metric, Black patients receive worse care than white patients. Their pain is taken less seriously. Their symptoms are more likely to be dismissed. Their outcomes are significantly worse, even when you control for income, education and access to care. As an example, in the UK, Black women are four times more likely to die from pregnancy or childbirth complications than white women.[22]

Four. Times.

This is not because of biology. It also has nothing to do with income or education level. It is because their pain and symptoms are more likely to be ignored.[23] In a famous example, Serena Williams almost died from giving birth. She had to beg for a CT scan and blood thinners after giving birth, despite having a known history of blood clots.[24] If a rich, famous athlete was not believed, imagine the odds for everyone else.

This pattern runs deep. In a 2016 study, half of white medical students and residents in the US falsely believed that Black people have thicker skin or less sensitive nerve endings. These are myths rooted in slavery that still shape how care is delivered today.[25,26] This is compounded by a general lack of funding into research and training to close this disparity for women of colour, with white skin still being treated as the default in Western medical training.

The history of 'bicycle face'

In the late 19th century, reports of a strange 'medical condition' began to circulate in newspapers and medical journals: *bicycle face.* It was described as the pale, tired, strained expression that supposedly impacted women who dared to ride bicycles. Doctors claimed that cycling would leave women with bulging eyes, flushed skin, tight jaws and even permanent facial disfigurement. Some went so far as to warn that too much cycling could cause infertility or hysteria.

Of course, none of this was true. The so-called bicycle face was not a medical condition at all, it was a social invention. For the first time, women could travel freely without needing a man, a horse or a carriage. Cycling became a symbol of independence and autonomy. And that terrified the patriarchy.

So, the myth of the bicycle face was created to scare women out of riding. It was part of a broader cultural backlash aimed at keeping women in their place, discouraging them from moving too far, too fast or too freely. The bicycle threatened to unshackle women from domestic confines, and so society responded with fearmongering disguised as medicine.

The story of bicycle face reminds us that throughout

history, women's health has often been weaponised against them. Myths, pseudo-science and false 'medical advice' have repeatedly been used to control women's bodies, choices and freedoms. While bicycle face may sound laughable today, the underlying pattern of using health as a tool to hold women back is anything but funny.[27–29]

UNSAFE BY DESIGN

Imagine this: You're prescribed medication. You take it exactly as instructed. But instead of feeling better, your symptoms worsen. You develop side effects no one warned you about. You return to the doctor, only to be told 'That's strange, this drug usually works fine.'

What they don't mention is this: it was never properly tested on someone like you.

The issues that women face in healthcare systems are rarely due to individual doctors and practitioners. Rather, it's because doctors are operating within a system that has been built on a biased foundation. For most of modern medical history, the female body has been treated as a scientific afterthought. In fact, until 1993 – yes, *1993* – the inclusion of women in clinical trials wasn't even part of US law.[30] As a result, the vast majority of medications used today were developed and tested on men. The male body was considered the default. The female body was seen as a complication.

Although official guidelines have changed in most countries, the legacy of this approach still shapes medicine today. Because when it comes to clinical research and funding, women continue to be left behind. Most animal studies are still done on male animals. Most human studies still have disproportionately more male participants.

That's a problem, because women respond differently to medication. Our bodies absorb and break down drugs in ways that men's bodies do not.[31,32] We have different hormone levels, different immune responses, different side-effect risks. Yet, the average dose is almost always calculated for a man. As a result, women are far more likely to experience side effects, to overdose, or to find that a drug simply doesn't work at all.

And it doesn't end there.

Even when a condition mostly affects women, the research still centres on men. Chronic pain is one of the clearest examples of this. Around 70% of people who live with chronic pain are women, yet 80% of pain studies are done on men or male animals.[33]

What gets funded gets fixed

At Female Invest, we often say that money is power. That's true on a personal level, and it's also true when you zoom out. Because in the world of medicine, what gets funded is what gets fixed. And the reality is that, globally, less than 5% of research and development funding is directed at female-specific conditions. This is split into 4% for female cancers and just 1% going to non-cancer conditions.[34] In the UK, less than 2.5% of publicly funded medical research goes towards reproductive health, despite the fact that one in three women will experience a reproductive or gynaecological health issue in her lifetime. Meanwhile, erectile dysfunction, which affects just 19% of men, receives five times more research funding than premenstrual syndrome, a condition that affects 90% of women.[35,36]

Even the private sector, driven by profits, has failed to catch up. A McKinsey analysis found that start-ups focused on erectile dysfunction received six times more funding than those working on endometriosis, despite the fact that the markets have similar size.[37,38] Yet funding continues to flow elsewhere, not because there isn't demand, not because the need isn't real, but because women's health still isn't treated as urgent.

Not painful enough. Not profitable enough. Not important enough.

Why doesn't this change?

The logic is as brutal as it is simple: What gets measured gets funded. What gets funded gets studied. What gets studied gets solved. And women's health is still left out of that loop.

Does this make you angry?

It should.

Realistically, every woman reading this will experience medical bias in her lifetime. Maybe it will be a doctor who dismisses your pain. Maybe it will be a drug that was never tested on someone like you. Maybe it will be an illness with no cure. Not because it's rare, but perhaps because it mostly affects women and research is underfunded.

The gap between men and women's healthy life expectancy isn't biological. It's structural. And it's expensive, for everyone.

Hysteria: The diagnosis used to silence millions of women

Medicine wasn't just made *for* men, it's been weaponised *against* women for centuries. The story of hysteria is a glaring example.

The word *hysteria* comes from the Greek word *hystera*, meaning uterus.[39] Male doctors in the eighteenth and nineteenth centuries believed a woman's womb could wander through her body, causing everything from anxiety to full-blown insanity.[40] The 'cure'? Sex (voluntary or rape). Pregnancy. Or if that didn't work: surgery.

You didn't have to be unwell to be diagnosed. Just angry, loud, ambitious, depressed, refusing sex or being too sexually independent. You could also be deemed hysterical for reading too much, disagreeing with your husband or feeling tired after giving birth. By the 19th century, 'tears and laughter' was enough to raise suspicions. Disobedience wasn't just discouraged, it was medicalised.[41]

Real treatments included removing the (healthy) uterus, brain surgery,[42] electroshock therapy,[43] months of isolation and forced sex (rape) or pregnancy.[44–46]

In 1860s France, one doctor claimed he could cure hysteria by manually massaging the genitals of female patients to 'release pressure' – a practice that would later inspire the invention of the vibrator.[47]

In the US and Europe, men could commit women to mental asylums with no trial. Just a husband's or father's signature. Real reasons included everything from 'refusing to keep house' to 'novel reading'. An official 19th-century asylum listed reasons such as 'political excitement', 'laziness' and 'imaginary female trouble'.[48]

In other words: women who didn't obey the men in their lives risked getting locked away.

It was never about health. It was about power, and it worked. By pathologising defiance, society turned ordinary women into patients and stripped them of credibility.

Sadly, this didn't stop in the Victorian era. In the 1950s, women were still being lobotomised[49] for 'nervousness' or 'promiscuity'.[50] In the 1960s, Valium became the top-selling drug in the US, nicknamed 'mother's little helper' for a reason.[51] It kept housewives calm and compliant.

Even today, the echoes remain. Women are twice as likely to be diagnosed with anxiety, and far less likely to be believed when reporting pain. Their symptoms are still brushed off as emotional, exaggerated or stress-related. We like to think we've moved on from the days of wandering wombs and mental asylums, but the truth is, modern medicine still often treats women's bodies and voices as unreliable.

When science is shaped by patriarchy, the goal isn't always to heal. It is also to silence.

WOMEN PAY THE PRICE

As it stands, we accept that women will spend more years in pain, on medication and out of work. That they'll chase answers through a healthcare system not built for them. That they'll keep footing the bill for the system's blind spots, with time, energy and with their quality of life.

For most of modern history, women's health has been defined by what it costs to treat. Rarely by what it costs to ignore.

But it might be worth considering, because when women are overlooked by the healthcare system, the damage of their pain and delayed diagnoses creates a cost. A real, measurable, financial cost – for individual women and for society. While it's often invisible in spreadsheets and headlines, it shows up in everyday life. In the sick days taken, the jobs lost, the hours spent chasing referrals. The side effects from drugs that weren't tested on women and the private appointments booked out of desperation when public waiting lists stretch into months. The endless juggling between pain and performance. Financially speaking, the cost of this poor health impacts women in three distinct ways:

1. Our ability to make money
2. Our ability to manage money
3. The direct costs we have to pay.

Our ability to *make* money

When your health declines, your income tends to follow. For millions of women around the world, this isn't just an occasional frustration, it's a recurring financial penalty that starts early and compounds over time, yet it's largely invisible in economic debates.

It's commonly assumed that this health burden is concentrated in our retirement years, but women actually spend more time living in ill health throughout their working years.[52] In a UK survey of over 60,000 women, 62% had experienced a period of poor health while at work.[53] One in four said it had directly impacted their earnings, and another 25% said it had cost them promotions. Even more worryingly, 22% said poor health forced them to leave the workforce earlier than planned.[54] Similarly, in the US, nearly one-third of working women say health issues have negatively affected their careers, and 15% say they've had to reduce their hours or stop working altogether.[55,56] Long-term illness is the most common reason for working-aged women being economically inactive, and this has real consequences.[57] The toll gets heavier in midlife. Perimenopause, endometriosis, autoimmune disorders and other chronic conditions often appear or intensify in these years – many of them still misunderstood or underdiagnosed.

These aren't minor setbacks, they're career-altering consequences and have massive economic implications. To put this into a wider context, every year UK businesses lose an estimated 150 million working days due to women's health issues, the equivalent of more than 500,000 full-time jobs.[58] That's half a million people effectively out of the workforce. Not because women don't want to work, but because the system around them isn't built to keep them well. It's estimated that reproductive health conditions like endometriosis, period pain and pelvic pain cost the UK economy £11 billion every year due to lost working days.[59] And in the US, a Deloitte report published in 2023 found that US employers lose over $26 billion annually due to lost productivity linked to women's health issues.[60]

A 2024 report by McKinsey and the World Economic Forum found that closing the women's health gap (including, but going far beyond, reproductive care) could unlock over $1 trillion in global GDP by 2040. Not by demanding *more* from women, but simply by reducing the years they spend in untreated or preventable illness. That's the equivalent of 137 million more women contributing fully to the workforce. For every $1 invested in women's health, the economy would gain at least $3.[61]

This is not a niche issue. It's an economic lever. But instead of pulling it, we waste it, in healthcare systems that dismiss women's pain and in workplaces that penalise women for being unwell. In governments that fail to fund research, that reflects half the population.

For self-employed women, the financial risk is even bigger. There's often no safety net, no paid sick leave and no income protection. When I was diagnosed with uveitis, and I couldn't look at screens for weeks, every hour of lost work meant lost revenue. Deadlines slipped. Projects paused. Still, I was lucky:

I had co-founders who could step in so I could afford to slow down, even if only temporarily. Many women can't. In countries without robust healthcare systems or workplace protections, the burden falls entirely on the individual.

And the problem compounds: lower earnings today means fewer contributions to pensions, reduced savings and less financial stability in the future. Poor health makes it harder to earn, and that has ripple effects across a woman's entire financial life.

Our ability to *manage* money

For anyone dealing with chronic health issues, managing the impact of that on their life is a huge and time-consuming endeavour. Just getting through the day, juggling symptoms, appointments, medications and the resulting admin, can consume so much energy that there's little left for anything else. Financial management quickly slips down the priority list. Not because it's unimportant, but because it becomes yet another source of stress in an already overloaded life.

And if there is one thing we know at Female Invest, it is that managing money requires time, headspace and routine: three things that chronic illness often takes away.

On top of that, poor health often comes with unpredictable costs – new medications, transport to appointments, therapy, specialist consultations – that make it difficult to keep track of what's going out, let alone plan what's left. This financial unpredictability adds to the mental load, making it harder to stay on top of budgets or make confident decisions.

The direct costs we have to pay

Globally speaking, staying healthy costs more if you're a woman.[62]

Preventative care is a clear example. Screenings like pap smears and mammograms often come with hidden fees – for appointments, follow-ups, or care outside public hours. Even when covered, many women still lose money taking time off work or travelling to access care.

Then there's contraception. Though essential, it's often treated as optional. In the UK, women spend an average of £250 a year on birth control. In the US, costs can run into the hundreds annually, with many insurance plans still not covering the full amount.

If a woman chooses to have children? The costs spike again. In many countries, even routine pregnancy check-ups, giving birth and postpartum care aren't fully covered by public healthcare.

Having insurance doesn't close the gap either. In the US, women pay around 20% more than men for coverage (and that's excluding pregnancy, which adds another $2,900 in out-of-pocket costs on average).[63]

It doesn't end there. Women are more likely to seek private care when they're not taken seriously or when waiting times are too long. At the time of writing, there are currently 760,000+ women waiting for NHS gynaecological appointments. If they were to stand in a line, the queue would go from London to Exeter (196 miles/315 km).[64] Putting aside the fact that I get sweaty palms if any queue has more than five people in it, I fully understand why women would seek private care when waiting times are this long. And they do.

In fact, UK women spend 1.5 times more than men on private healthcare (around £305 per year), despite earning less.[65] As a result, in total women spend about £1.5 billion more on healthcare annually than men. Unsurprisingly, this difference is particularly pronounced in areas of fertility, menopause and menstrual health, but women also spend 25% more on general healthcare, such as dental care, physiotherapy and private GP visits.[66]

It's clear that the gender health gap doesn't just impact women's quality of life. It also impacts our ability to make and manage money, while adding tangible costs that are often unavoidable. When women's health is neglected, economies shrink. The cost of inaction is staggering, but the opportunity is even greater. By prioritising research, funding and care that reflects women's lived realities, we don't just improve health outcomes, we unlock economic growth, innovation and equality. Investing in women's health is no longer a moral imperative alone. It's a smart policy. It's sound economics. And it's long overdue.

The Chainsaw Was Invented for Women

Every now and then, history gifts us a medical invention developed specifically for women. One such invention stands out for all the wrong reasons: the chainsaw. In the late 18th century, two Scottish surgeons, John Aitken and James Jeffray, designed a chainsaw to make childbirth 'easier'. Before caesarean sections were common, doctors relied on a procedure called *symphysiotomy* when a baby was stuck in the birth canal. Instead of opening the abdomen, they sawed through the mother's pelvic bone to widen it, often while she was fully conscious. The chainsaw made this gruesome task faster and 'more efficient'. Its design was based on a watch chain with teeth that moved using a hand-crank. This meant that, although the mother may not have looked down to see her doctor holding a version of the chainsaw we know today, she would see her doctor furiously cranking a chainsaw against her vulva. Again, often without any anaesthesia.

The practice spread across Europe and was still performed on women well into the 20th century, especially in Ireland, where hundreds underwent it as late as the 1980s. The procedure often had catastrophic health consequences, and in 2014 a group of survivors filed a complaint against the Irish Government to the UN Human Rights Committee. Here, they recounted some of their horrifying experiences:

'I couldn't see much except for them sawing. It was excruciating pain,' recalled a patient who gave birth to her third child in 1959, 'I was just 27 and I was butchered.'

So where does this leave us today? The chainsaw was mechanised in the late 19th century to increase its ease of use by OB/GYNs on expectant mothers. This led to the mechanised chainsaw eventually getting adopted by the timber industry in 1905, allowing the instrument to be applied to trees, rather than its original use on women. Something to think about next time you see a chainsaw in use.[67]

THE BEST INVESTMENT YOU WILL EVER MAKE

Through our work in Female Invest, we spend a lot of time talking about the importance of investing your money in assets and building wealth over time. But the truth is: the most important investment you'll ever make is in yourself, and your physical and mental well-being.

Why? Because that's the foundation of everything else.

It's so easy to deprioritise, especially as women, when our role has historically been to care for others before caring for ourselves. But here's the thing: we can't show up for others if we don't show up for ourselves first.

We've had to learn this the hard way. When starting Female Invest, we got consumed by a mission bigger than ourselves. As a result, we worked around the clock, and at some points even sleep became an inconvenience. We lost friendships and relationships, but we kept going and never looked back, because we knew we were building towards a better future. What we didn't realise, until it was too late, was that we also lost our health.

Within a few years, we went from being healthy to struggling with autoimmune disease, migraines and crippling anxiety. Sleep went out the window, we deprioritised exercise and our diet consisted of whatever took the least time to prepare and eat. The costs of this lifestyle meant we suffered, and our business did too. We spent too much time being sick, not functioning at our highest level.

Two years ago, we hit a breaking point and decided to turn things around and start investing in our health. Here, the obsessive part of our personalities came in handy, because it enabled us to go *all in*. We changed our diets *completely* and educated ourselves on diet, sleep, exercise and supplements through podcasts, books and wearing devices to track our blood sugar and stress levels in real time and we even had blood tests done to know exactly which areas to focus on. The results were remarkable.

Within a few months, our anxiety decreased, we slept better and started having more energy. And within the first year, migraines became an exception rather than the default in particularly intense periods. It's still not perfect, and we are learning every day, but our lives look completely different from before.

But it required big investments. We've invested a lot of time in learning about health, and we continue to put in many hours every week in food prepping, bedtime routine and exercising. We've also invested a lot of money in tests, wearable tracking devices, gym memberships, high-quality food, supplements and therapy. And we're not alone in this: women spend 10% more than men on medical diagnostics and wearable devices. It's a massive privilege to afford such things, and this burden should not be placed on the individual. But until society catches up and starts prioritising prevention, we have decided there is nothing better to spend our money on. It is a financial investment that will likely continue for the rest of our lives, and forever be something we prioritise in our budgets.

I sometimes get comments like '*make sure it doesn't take over your life*' or '*it's also important to live a little*'. And I can't help but wonder: why are many people so afraid to openly and proudly invest in their health? And does choosing a mocktail on a night out really mean that you miss out?

Having experienced the consequences of poor health first-hand, I can confidently say: nothing makes you miss out on life more than being sick. For women especially, being your own health advocate is essential. We live in systems that weren't designed for us: medical research, clinical guidelines, even workplace policies. That means we can't rely on anyone else to prioritise our health. We have to do it ourselves.

Here's what that can look like:

- **Make prevention your baseline**. Prioritise check-ups, nutritious food, movement, sleep and stress reduction. It's not glamorous, but prevention is always cheaper – financially and emotionally – than treatment.
- **Buy long-term health insurance while you're young and healthy**. It's easier and cheaper before health issues arise. If you're older or divorced, qualifying becomes harder and

premiums climb fast. Securing it early gives you protection when you need it most.

- **Build a health emergency fund**. Unexpected costs (from dental surgery to therapy, fertility treatment or hormone support) can appear overnight. Having savings set aside ensures you can get care when you need it, without financial stress.

Just after closing our Series A, our biggest funding round at the time of writing, I felt the familiar pain return behind my left eye. It had been more than four years since my first uveitis episode, and I had started to believe I was in the clear. But just days after signing the papers, my eye doctor confirmed what I already feared: the uveitis was back.

What followed was six relentless months of flare-ups. I bounced between private doctors and the emergency room at the eye hospital, where I've cried in the reception more times than I'd like to admit. It wasn't easier this second time around. If anything, it was worse – mentally, emotionally and physically. Once again, I was trapped in the same awful calculation: treat the inflammation and risk serious side effects or leave it untreated, which results in certain blindness.

For those unfamiliar, uveitis is treated with steroid eye drops that, over time, can cause blindness for a range of different reasons. One common reason is increased pressure inside the eye. That's dangerous, because elevated eye pressure can lead to glaucoma, which can also cause irreversible blindness.

At first, I was lucky. For months, my eye pressure stayed within a safe range, and I told myself I was in the clear. But after five months with repeated uveitis episodes, everything changed. Between two appointments, the pressure in my eye had doubled. This time, I didn't need a doctor to tell me something was wrong. I could feel it. A dull, intense pain, getting worse towards the evening, making it hard to focus on anything else.

I knew exactly what high eye pressure could mean. I'd done the research. I'd asked the questions. At my appointment, my doctor confirmed my fears. This was not looking good, and continuing with the eye drops would only make matters worse, but there were no other treatment options.

I remember bawling my eyes out in the hospital's hallway after that appointment. (Which ironically made the pain even worse, because crying temporarily increases eye pressure too.) As I broke down in the hallway, a nurse came, sat down with me and put her arm around me. She didn't offer any words of comfort, but I guess there weren't really any to give.

It's hard to describe how wrong it feels to knowingly take medication that could damage your body. To drip your hurting eye up to fifteen times per day with liquid that can make you blind, knowing that every drop increases the risk of irreversible damage. But I had no real choice. Uveitis *guarantees* blindness if left untreated. The medication only *might* cause it.

It was a brutal, no-win situation. And once again, it came at a terrible time.

One of my co-founders had just given birth and was on maternity leave, the other was heavily pregnant. We missed deadlines, had to pause major projects, and even pushed the writing of this book. When your health fails, everything else does too. No matter how strong your will is.

It's hard to say exactly how much it cost our company, but the price of missed deadlines, flatlined growth and 30+ employees who still need a salary but lack direction from leadership is not cheap. It also cost me on a personal level: in the past year, I've spent more than £7,000 on private eye doctors (because public waiting times were too long), medication and various health checks. I'm lucky enough to live just around the corner from the UK's best private eye hospital. Still, when I initially heard the price of treatment my gut instinct was to say 'I can't afford that'. But then I thought twice, and accepted that the only thing I truly *can't* afford is losing my vision.

I ended up being 'lucky' once again. My uveitis cleared up, and I still have intact vision on both eyes. But the steroid drops have left me with damage to my left eye: scarring, pain and increased light sensitivity. As I write this chapter, I am still in and out of eye doctor appointments, trying to figure out if this damage is permanent and how to treat it.

Through my health checks, I also learnt that I carry a really crappy gene that significantly increases my risk for a long list of autoimmune diseases like uveitis. So who knows – maybe I will end up as just another statistic in this chapter: yet another woman who could have had an incredible career, made a positive difference in the world and generated a lot of money in the process, only to see her career, healthspan and financial capacity cut short because of chronic disease. Even the most driven person is only as unstoppable as their health allows.

As I round off this chapter, there's one message I want to underline: investing in your health is a financial strategy. Too often, we separate the two – as if health is a luxury item. But the reality is: your health is your earning power. It's your ability to work, lead, think clearly, make good decisions and build a life on your terms. Neglecting it comes at a cost, and you can't avoid the bill.

This doesn't mean living perfectly. We definitely don't. But it does mean backing yourself. It means doing your best, taking yourself seriously and being fine with 'missing out' on things that don't serve you, whether it's habits, food or people. And most of all, it means choosing long-term well-being over short-term comfort.

When your health is strong, you can show up for your family, your career, your goals and your future. You can work smarter, longer and more efficiently. For us, investing in our health has been one of the best financial decisions we've ever made, both personally and professionally.

Your health isn't a side project or an afterthought, it's a core pillar of your financial foundation. Take it seriously. Prioritise it now. Because when women thrive, we don't just feel better. We do better. We earn more, lead more, and build the futures we deserve.

MONEY AND MOTHER-HOOD

By Camilla

Motherhood is incredible, but in today's world it often comes with devastating financial consequences. Because for most women, the biggest glass ceiling isn't found at the office – it's found in the rigid expectations of motherhood. If you aren't careful, maternity leave won't just be a break from work: it will be the break that breaks your financial future.

FACT SHEET

- Mothers earn 30–40% less than childless women in the decade after childbirth.[1]

- Fathers earn 23% more than childless men.[2]

- Despite 98% of UK mothers wanting to go back to work after having children, only 24% go back full time.[3]

- Mothers typically see a pension savings decrease of £92,000–£183,000.[4]

- Every year, around 74,000 women in the UK lose their jobs during pregnancy or maternity leave.[5]

Nine months of relentless nausea and puking. Seventeen hours of labour. An emergency suction delivery. A third-degree tear.

When I finally held my baby in my arms, I thought the hardest part was behind me. I was exhausted, stitched up and barely able to move – but I was overflowing with love. Surely, the hard part was over.

I was wrong.

What came next wasn't just about healing my body, although that was a part of it: it was about learning to navigate an entirely new reality. Like so many women before me, I suddenly had to figure out how to juggle motherhood, work and money, all while running on no sleep and keeping a newborn alive. There was no road map. No onboarding. Just an overwhelming sense that I was supposed to hold it all together.

That's why I've written this chapter. When it comes to motherhood and money, most of us are flying blind. No one teaches us how maternity leave affects our career, how unpaid care work drains our pensions, or how easily modern couples slip into old-school gender roles, often without ever choosing them. We're told to follow our instincts, but instincts can't protect you from a financial system that punishes mothers and rewards fathers.

I want to warn you that this chapter might be a hard one to read, because it challenges many narratives around motherhood that we're brought up to believe. At the same time, I want to be clear that we are not here to judge your choices: we want to make sure you understand the full picture. When reading it, please keep in mind that this isn't about whether or not to have children. Only you can make that decision, and it's a decision that involves your whole life, not only the financial side. We're also not saying that having children is bad. In fact, at the time of writing, we have three children between the three of us. Rather, the purpose of this chapter is to educate you on the financial challenges and opportunities of motherhood, because you can't make an informed decision if you've never been given the information.

THE MOTHERHOOD PENALTY

As a mother, I know how motherhood can be a transformative and meaningful experience. It brings moments of profound joy, deep connection and a sense of purpose that shapes every part of life. At its best, it can expand your perspective and fill your days with love in ways you never imagined. But it also comes with major financial consequences, and we need to talk about them.

These challenges are part of a broader pattern known as the 'motherhood penalty'. This refers to the systematic disadvantages women face when having children, and the consequences last a lifetime. They impact women's earnings, career progression and future pension in ways that are rarely acknowledged or fairly compensated.

The first barrier: pregnancy

While every woman's journey is different, the pattern is painfully predictable, and it starts with pregnancy.

On one hand, pregnancy marks the beginning of an exciting new chapter. It's a time filled with anticipation, little milestones and the joy of imagining the life ahead. But in the workplace, it can feel like the beginning of the end: of momentum, of promotions, of people believing that you are committed to your work. We all know that the physical toll of pregnancy is significant, but what's often overlooked is how financially and professionally destabilising it can be.

There are the obvious factors: doctor's appointments, scans, midwife visits and unexpected complications, all of which often require time off that's either unpaid or quietly penalised. A 2025 study found that over 74,000 women a year in the UK lose their jobs during pregnancy or maternity leave.[6] And many more report subtle sidelining: important meetings scheduled without them and promotions delayed or denied.[7,8]

Then there's the cost of being pregnant. In countries without universal healthcare, out-of-pocket costs can be high. In the US, the average cost of childbirth is $18,865 for vaginal delivery and $26,280 for a C-section.[9] These figures only refer to the delivery process and don't include the time off work, the cost of prenatal supplements, maternity clothing or the early baby essentials families start buying before the baby even arrives.

The cost of maternity leave

Then comes maternity leave, which, while absolutely essential, is one of the most misunderstood drivers of the motherhood penalty. What is often described as a 'break from work' is in fact a period of intense, unpaid labour. Mothers are up at all hours feeding, healing, surviving, while nurturing the next generation of taxpayers.

And financially, the costs of maternity leave are high.

According to the OECD, only 36% of countries offer full-rate equivalent maternity pay for more than fourteen weeks.[10] In many countries, like the US, there's no national paid maternity leave at all, pushing many women to use up vacation days, take unpaid leave or quit their job.

Even in the UK, where statutory maternity leave lasts up to fifty-two weeks, only the first six weeks are paid at 90% of your salary. The remaining thirty-three weeks are paid at *either* £187 per week or 90% of your average weekly earnings (whichever is *lower*),[11] which is barely enough to cover rent in most cities. And for women in countries where maternity leave is unpaid or patchy, it's even worse.

The three of us are from Denmark, often hailed as one of the most progressive countries in the world when it comes to parental leave. Yet even with 10.5 months of national paid parental leave that can be shared by the parents regardless of gender, research by economist Henrik Kleven shows that it is women's earnings that drop sharply after their first child, and never recover. Over time, this gap widens. Kleven concluded that 80% of Denmark's gender wage gap is directly linked to motherhood (see graph on the opposite page, above).[12]

His work also found that women without children tend to earn salaries comparable to men, but once children enter the picture, the divergence is immediate and it rarely closes (see graph on the opposite page, below).

Denmark, remember, is today's best-case scenario. In other countries, where policies are weaker and childcare is more expensive, the gap is even wider.

So what does this mean? The gender wage gap is often just a motherhood penalty in disguise. And maternity leave easily ends up being the career break that breaks your career.

Compare that to fathers. In 2023, US data showed that fathers

Earnings inequality for first-time parents

A first child impacts a woman's earnings dramatically, whereas a man's earnings remain unchanged

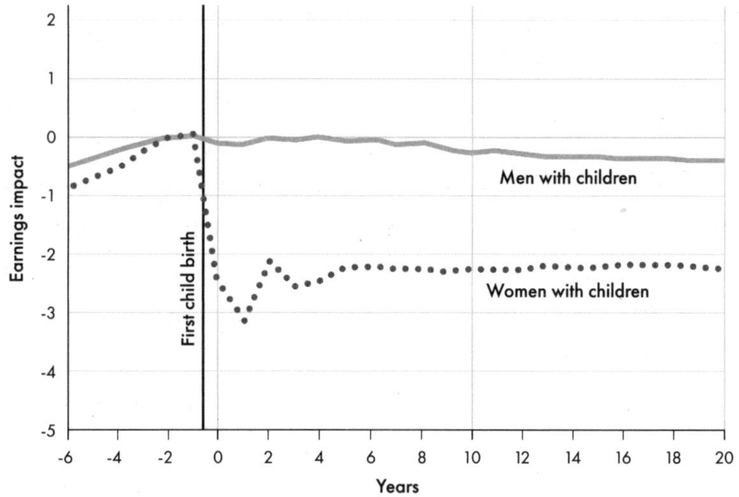

Source: 'Children and gender inequality: Evidence from Denmark', National Bureau of Economic Research (2018).[13]

Women with children earn less than women without children

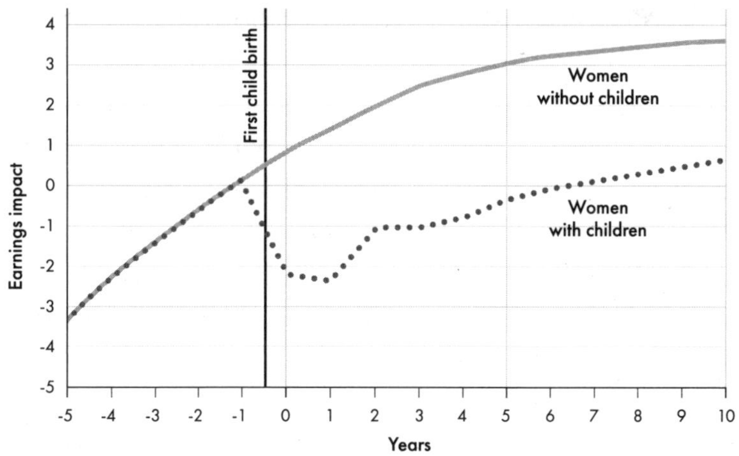

Source: 'Children and gender inequality: Evidence from Denmark', National Bureau of Economic Research (2018).[14]

with children earned 23% *more* than their childless counterparts.[15] This phenomenon is known as the 'fatherhood bonus', and it's because fathers are seen as more committed and stable at work, while mothers are viewed as the opposite.[16]

I hate to say it, but there might be some truth to this. Anyone with children knows that with a new baby comes new responsibilities at home, from more domestic labour to a bigger mental load. Cleaning, washing, cooking, scheduling doctor's appointments, keeping track of vaccinations, remembering what size shoes the kids wear, packing school bags, buying birthday presents, arranging childcare, meal planning, signing permission slips, booking swimming lessons, and anticipating everything the household needs before anyone else even notices.

I don't blame you if you zoned out halfway through that list. It's overwhelming to read it – let alone *live* it. If two parents shared these responsibilities equally, it might not destroy the woman's career and finances, but in heterosexual relationships, that's often not the case. On average, women do ten more hours of unpaid, domestic work per week than their male partner.[17]

So while we (for good reason) often blame employers for not doing enough to help new mums, we might miss the underlying reason why mothers earn less and progress slower in their career: the father of their children. Or rather, the unspoken expectations rooted in traditional gender roles that many couples adopt without making a deliberate decision about it. Equality in the workplace starts with equality at home, and if fathers did their part of the work, mothers wouldn't suffer financially for a lifetime. The real obstacle to your financial future might not (only) be your boss, but the person you share a bed with. Of course, every couple can decide what division of labour works for them. But we urge you to have upfront conversations about it, to avoid slipping into traditional gender roles simply because that's the way it has always been.

The return to work (or not)

Based on this unfair division of labour, it's not surprising that many mothers move into lower-paid part-time roles to make it all work. In the UK, 17% of women leave work completely within five years of childbirth, compared to just 4% of men.[18]

It makes sense: if you're expected to take the entirety of parental leave, studies show your career will likely stall. If you return only to find you've become the default parent juggling logistics, remembering birthdays, scheduling doctor's appointments, it impacts everything: your energy, your visibility, your ability to move up.

Outsourcing this new labour often isn't feasible. In fact, another reason why women are pushed out of paid work is the eye-watering cost of childcare. In the UK, full-time childcare costs an average of £14,000 per year; in Australia, families spend an average of 26% of household income on childcare,[19] and in Germany, where childcare is subsidised, access is patchy and likely part of why 66% of mothers work part time.[20]

Here's the thing, though: when women step down from their paid jobs – even if it makes sense in the short term to avoid childcare costs – it has serious long-term implications. Lower earnings and time out of the workforce mean lower pensions, fewer savings and reduced financial security later in life. In the EU, the gender pension gap is currently around 29%. In the UK, mothers face an estimated pension penalty of up to £183,000.[21] Similarly in Germany, women retire with pensions that are on average 46% lower than men's, largely because of unpaid caregiving.[22]

That's how the motherhood penalty compounds over time: not just in lost wages today, but in the wealth gap tomorrow.

WHEN SOCIETAL NORMS MAKE THE DECISIONS FOR YOU

One of our members, Marie, recently shared her story with me. From the start, Marie did everything right. Straight out of business school, she landed her dream job as a sustainability consultant at a major bank in London. She worked hard, delivered results, and was promoted twice in record time. By the time she left for maternity leave, she was a manager earning the equivalent of £7,600 a month.

Like many women, Marie took the majority of parental leave and spent eight months at home with her newborn. Three months with full pay, five months with no pay. When she returned to work, she didn't receive the promotion she had been on track for, while her husband (who works at the same bank in a similar role) was promoted and given a raise equivalent to £1,400 per month.

Layered on top of that is the invisible labour she found herself taking on: Marie manages nearly all the work at home, including both drop-offs and pick-ups of their now eighteen-month-old daughter. That means she can't stay late in the office, take on extra hours or stretch for those high-visibility projects in the way some of her colleagues can.

So how much did Marie's eight months of maternity leave cost her?
Let's break it down:

- **Missed salary:** She missed out on £38,000 in salary during her five months of unpaid leave (that's £7,600 × 5 months).

- **Missed pension:** She missed out on pension contributions worth £3,040 (that's 8% of her salary over those five unpaid months). Over time, that missing contribution realistically would have grown to £30,590 by the time she turns 60.[23]
- **Total loss:** £38,000 salary + £30,590 retirement = £68,590.

The calculation does not take into account the potential salary increase of £1,400 per month that she would have received had she got a promotion like her husband.

For the sake of simplicity, let's assume that she gets £1,400 less than her male counterparts every month for the rest of her career. This might sound drastic, but it's actually very realistic. Why? Because at every salary negotiation going forward, she will have a lower starting point – and that's assuming she even gets back on the same career track. Statistically, she is more likely to move to a lower-paying job to balance out the unpaid labour at home.

So with the conservative assumption that she 'only' misses out on £1,400 per month, her total salary loss until retirement is:

£1,400 per month × 12 months = £16,800 per year

£16,800 per year × 30 years = £504,000

If she had invested this extra money and got the average market return of 8% per year, this would have grown to £1,903,157.

Suddenly, the cost of childcare doesn't seem so expensive, does it?

Marie's partner isn't some villain who set out to benefit financially from her maternity leave or the imbalance at home. It wasn't calculated. It just . . . happened. Neither of them paused to ask the hard questions.

There were assumptions, good intentions and a thousand small defaults that slowly became a pattern. And suddenly, a year had passed – and Marie felt more depleted than ever. Financially. Emotionally. There was little energy left to come back to work at full speed, let alone keep climbing the corporate ladder. Nothing about their set-up had been malicious. But that's the thing about societal norms – when you don't actively question them, they quietly decide for you. No one had asked what this would mean for Marie's career, or her long-term financial well-being. By the time they realised it, the gap was already there and it felt impossible to close.

Of course, these numbers don't tell the whole story. Many women look at their male partners – their freedom, their uninterrupted income, their career momentum – and feel a mix of envy and frustration. But we don't often talk about what men miss out on too. Because what Marie gained, like so many women before her, is something profoundly meaningful. In a world obsessed with productivity, purpose rooted in family is powerful.

Still, none of that makes the trade-off easy. And it *is* a trade-off.

As a relatively new mother myself and co-founder of a start-up, I know this first-hand. I couldn't take a long maternity leave. When I told my friends and family I'd only be home with my son for a short time – much shorter than what's normal here in Denmark – I felt the mum guilt immediately. I felt judged by the people I loved. While I'm incredibly lucky that my husband's job offered a fully paid paternity leave, which meant it made sense for our family that he took the longer stretch, it still wasn't easy for me to return to work. I knew what I was missing out on at home.

So yes, I get the financial logic of returning to work fast. I also get the ache of wanting to stay home longer. Both feelings can live in the same body. What matters is making informed decisions and fully understanding the consequences of the choices you make, while being honest with yourself and with the person you're building a life with. When expectations are unspoken, when one partner quietly assumes the other will scale back without asking what that actually means, that's when the cracks start to show.

This isn't about judgement, or glorifying so-called hustle culture. If you want to be the primary caregiver, take the longer leave or run the household, that's a beautiful, empowering choice. My own parents had a traditional arrangement that worked wonderfully: my father worked full time, my mother raised four children and kept the home running with love and care. And I know many women who find deep purpose in that path.

But sadly, many women – including members of our community, including Marie – didn't actively choose the roles they ended up in. They assumed partnership meant equity, only to find that the day-to-day expectations told a different story. They didn't ask the questions. Perhaps they didn't want to seem difficult. Or high-maintenance. Or too ambitious. But avoiding hard conversations leads to living a much harder reality.

Every day. For the rest of your life.

And when 50% of marriages end in divorce? It does not look good.

HOW TO MITIGATE THE MOTHERHOOD PENALTY

Now that you understand the potential financial impact, here's the good news: knowledge is power. With the insights you've just gained, you're better equipped to make choices about your future. Yes, it might mean having some uncomfortable conversations with your partner – but avoiding them comes at a much higher cost. If your partner needs more context, ask them to read this chapter. It's not just your burden to carry.

This chapter will focus on what you as an individual can do. But let's be clear: this isn't only about personal choices, it's about a system that was never built with women in mind. We should all be asking the bigger question: what would it look like to properly support and value mothers? Ideas like universal basic income for mothers, or government-funded caregiver salaries, aren't radical: they're necessary. The unpaid labour of women underpins our entire economy. Without it, society would fall apart. And yet, mothers are often treated as an expense, rather than a cornerstone.

We should be demanding more: affordable childcare, paid parental leave that truly supports both parents, flexible workplaces and real financial recognition of caregiving. The goal isn't just to help women 'manage' within an unequal system: it's to redesign the system altogether. Change will come when enough of us demand it.

Until that happens, let's take a look at how you can mitigate the motherhood penalty in your own life.

8 steps to minimise the motherhood penalty

1. **Don't settle because you're stressed about the timeline**
If you find a wonderful partner who is willing to have a truly equal partnership – that's fantastic. But, sadly, too many women choose a subpar partner in their late twenties or early thirties, driven by societal pressure or fear of the biological clock. The pressure of time is real but shouldn't lead to a lifetime of being dragged down, of sacrificing your freedom, happiness, health and finances. As we explore in 'All the Single Ladies' and 'Married Men Are the Real Gold-diggers', staying single or choosing solo motherhood is far better than tying yourself to the wrong person. Choosing the father for your children is the biggest financial decision you will ever make – and one you can never undo.
2. **Invite the father to co-create your parenting approach**
Too often, mothers quietly take the lead on every parenting decision from nap times and meal choices to bedtime routines, discipline approaches and screen time limits. Fathers are left playing catch-up. It's not always intentional, but when one parent becomes the default decision-maker, the other can quickly start to feel like an intern. This imbalance doesn't just hurt him, it increases your load and undermines long-term equality. Invite your partner to be just as involved in shaping how your children are raised. That means researching together, talking through values and agreeing on the kind of parents you want to be as a team. Fatherhood isn't just a responsibility. It's an incredibly rewarding, identity-shaping experience. And it becomes even more filled with purpose, joy and connection when he's a co-pilot, not a bystander.

3. **Compensate the partner doing more domestic work**
   If you're staying home and not getting paid, your partner shouldn't only say thank you, they should pay up. You're covering the cost of childcare, cleaning, mental load and the emotional labour of keeping your family running. If you hired someone to do it, it would cost a fortune. In the UK, full-time childcare alone averages £14,000 per year per child,[24] and that doesn't include cleaning, laundry, cooking and so on, which would easily double that number. Financial compensation protects you from being punished for doing the essential work that keeps the household afloat.
4. **Top up the pension for the person taking unpaid leave**
   Taking time off to raise a child doesn't only impact your current income, it eats into your future wealth too. As we saw with Marie, even a single year off can cost tens of thousands in missed pension contributions and compound interest. If your partner is still working while you're doing unpaid labour, they should contribute to your pension. Why? Because their career is being built on your invisible work.
5. **Make sure the father takes parental leave**
   When men take leave, it normalises shared responsibility. When they don't, it reinforces outdated gender roles and leaves women shouldering the full burden of care. Studies show that when fathers take even short parental leave, they're more likely to stay involved long term.[25,26] In Iceland, where parental leave is shared and incentivised, 90% of fathers take leave.[27] In contrast, in countries where it's optional or culturally discouraged, uptake can be as low as 1%.[28]
6. **Don't take *all* parental leave at the same time**
   It sounds romantic: the two of you at home with a new

baby. But if the father is never left alone with the child, he never fully learns what it takes. It's you who ends up default-parenting for life. The most effective set-ups give dads solo time to figure it out themselves. According to a Swedish study, when fathers took at least thirty days of solo parental leave, mothers reported better mental health, stronger career recovery and more balanced household labour years later.[29] Overlap is fine, but separation is necessary if you want a chance for more equal caretaking.

7. **Ensure full visibility into household finances**

   Every person in a relationship should always know:
   - how much money is coming in (and from where);
   - how much is going out (and where it's going).

   Financial transparency isn't just about trust, it's about power. Women are more likely to experience financial abuse, and lack of insight into money is one of the biggest enablers. In a UK study, one in six women said they had experienced economic abuse, often without realising it, until it was too late.[30]

8. **Split costs based on income**

   Equal isn't always fair. If one person is earning significantly less (or nothing at all) during leave, expecting a 50/50 split on bills only makes the financial gap wider. If you are in a split-finances arrangement, we recommend that costs should be divided proportionally based on income, so that the person who's already giving up earnings isn't penalised twice. Globally, 72% of unpaid care work is done by women,[31] and yet they're still often expected to split household costs as if they weren't already subsidising the family and their husband's career with their time and unpaid work.

I'll never forget a conversation with a Female Invest member who told me she felt bad for using her husband's money while on maternity leave. This kind of thinking is the result of centuries of patriarchy training women to undervalue their own labour. She wasn't *using* his money. She was *subsidising* his career. Without her doing the invisible, unpaid work at home – caring for their child, keeping the household running – he wouldn't have been able to earn that salary in the first place.

Why is it that men's time is automatically seen as more valuable, while women are made to feel guilty for raising the children both parents created? Why are we so comfortable treating women's time, labour and bodies as infinite resources – and then acting like any man who changes a nappy deserves a standing ovation?

After birth, mothers often *do* take on the majority of childcare. Not because they're 'biologically better at it', but because systems, stereotypes and social pressure push them into it. Yes, research does show that women tend to be more attuned to their infants' cues and needs – but this is not because of biology, it's because they've spent more time doing the work and learning from it.[32,33]

Still, calling it a 'natural difference' is convenient. It gives men an easy excuse to opt out and keeps women locked into unpaid roles that quietly fuel their partners' careers. The so-called maternal instinct is often just practice, proximity and pressure. While it's totally fair if one parent *wants* to stay home more, we shouldn't confuse that with a *biological reason*.

Of course, only people in female bodies can biologically breastfeed, but that doesn't automatically mean that caregiving is the woman's role. Breastfeeding is just one aspect of a baby's early life, and even then, many families use formula, pumps or shared feeding routines that allow fathers and partners to step in. What truly builds bonds isn't breast milk alone. It's presence, comfort and consistency. Once feeding is done, everything from rocking the baby to midnight soothing and changing nappies can be shared equally. Reducing motherhood to breastfeeding overlooks the countless ways parents nurture, and it risks cementing the outdated idea that women are the 'default' caregivers.

The gap shrinks when fathers take on more responsibility. And this is where the journey towards equality starts.

Of course, everyone should choose the path that's right for them. As I said at the beginning, we are not here to shame anyone for staying at home. We are here to make sure you're fully informed when making that decision. The truth is, we're not taught this stuff growing up. No one sits you down and explains how easily gender roles can creep in, or how unpaid care work can quietly shape your entire financial future. Too often, couples slide into dynamics neither of them consciously chose. But the person who ends up paying the highest price in terms of freedom and finances is almost always the woman.

As I've learnt first-hand, there's no perfect solution, only trade-offs. No matter what path you choose, you'll likely carry guilt for what you're missing at home or what you're sacrificing at work. No matter what you choose, people will judge you. But you deserve to make the choice that is best for you with your eyes wide open.

UNWANTED PREGNANCY

The chapter about money and motherhood could have ended here. But it doesn't. Until now, we've done what most people do: assumed that pregnancy and motherhood is by default a happy and wanted circumstance.

The truth is that not all pregnancies are planned. And not all decisions feel like real choices.

We know it, because we lived it too.

Some years ago, one of us got pregnant, despite being on birth control. We'd rather not say who, but what you need to know is that pregnancy should have been impossible. Yet there it was: a second pink line staring back at her.

The moment the test turned positive, panic set in. Her chest tightened. Her thoughts scattered. She couldn't breathe. This wasn't a joyful revelation, it was terror, loneliness and disbelief all rolled into one.

She only told two people: her co-founders.

They didn't know what to say, only that they were going to be there for her.

At first, she decided on a medical abortion. She booked herself into a hotel room, determined to go through it alone. She didn't want anyone to see her like that – vulnerable, in pain.

That night was long. The cramps came in waves, pain shooting through her body. Her mind felt distant and foggy, like it had left her to cope on its own. She lay curled in a hotel bed, bleeding and crying, with no one there to hold her hand.

A week later, she went to her gynaecologist to make sure it was over.

It wasn't.

There was still tissue left inside her. Still pregnant, still stuck in limbo.

So she tried again. Another round of medication. More pain. More bleeding.

And then again.

Each time, she wanted it to end. Each time, it didn't.

Eventually, it was decided that she needed a surgical abortion.

One of her co-founders went with her.

It was dark when they arrived at the hospital. The world outside was sleeping. Inside, they curled up next to each other in a hospital bed, holding hands in the silence. They didn't talk much. They didn't need to.

The weeks leading up to it had been a living hell. Nausea. Pain. Shame. Fear. The burden of keeping it all a secret.

No one else knew they were there, and it felt like they were alone in this world.

When in fact, she found herself in a situation that 73 million women globally go through every year.[34]

Back at the hospital, she changed into a thin gown. It had already been hours of waiting – just like the day before, when they'd been sent home mid-abortion[35] because the hospital was understaffed.

Now it was finally time. She lay down on the operating table, quietly hoping this would be the end of it all. The end of the appointments, the uncertainty, the pain. As the anaesthesia took hold, she braced herself – physically and emotionally.

She woke up in excruciating, indescribable pain.

It was blinding, radiating through her abdomen like fire. The doctors were confused. At first, they thought they'd punctured her uterus. But soon they realised that she'd contracted a serious pelvic inflammatory disease.

It lasted for weeks after the surgery. The pain didn't just come in waves, it never left. Standing upright became a struggle. Walking was too painful.

But she didn't have the luxury of falling apart, because no one knew. Not her colleagues, not her friends, not even her family. So she smiled through investor meetings. She hosted team calls while curled up in a chair, fists clenched under the table. She led strategy sessions while quietly bleeding.

Why are we sharing this? To underline that abortion is

healthcare. That anyone can end up needing one, and that going through it is not easy.

The only thing that was easy about the abortion was the decision to have it.

Because becoming a mother is a life-altering experience. And if it happens at the wrong time, with the wrong partner, or before you're ready – emotionally, mentally or financially – it doesn't just shift your future. It can shatter it.

A BABY IS NOT ALWAYS A BLESSING

Many of us might have grown up hearing that 'a baby is always a blessing'. But when we look at the numbers, they tell a different story.

Most women who seek abortions are already living on low incomes.[36] When they're denied that choice, the consequences are devastating. Research is clear: women who are forced to carry unwanted pregnancies face a sharp decline in financial stability. Poverty increases, full-time employment drops and families are more likely to fall below the poverty line.[37–39]

A study by the University of Chicago confirmed that unplanned pregnancies have substantial, negative and lasting consequences on the careers of previously childless women. Within six years of having an unplanned child, women earn 20% less than if their unplanned pregnancy had not occurred.[40]

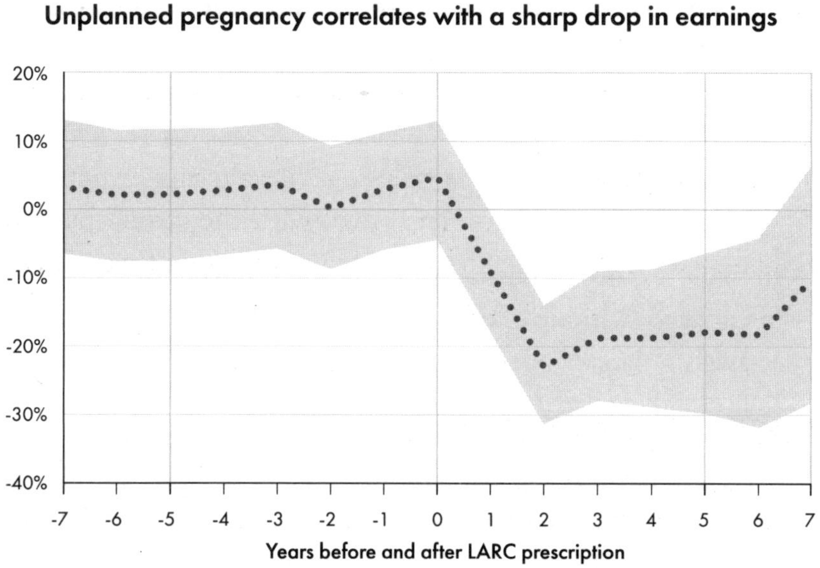

Source: Becker Friedman Institute (2023). This graph This graph demonstrates the impact of unplanned pregnancy on earnings including paid leave by time alter a Long-Acting Reversible Contraception (LARC) prescription in Sweden. Income is measured in hundred thousands of 2010 Swedish Kroka (SEK). The shaded area represents the 95% confidence interval.[41]

Even for privileged women, like ourselves, an unplanned pregnancy at the wrong time is life-altering. Our abortion story happened in the early days of Female Invest. Without the ability to make that choice, the company likely wouldn't exist today. Our careers, our independence and even the relationships we're in now – with partners we *chose* and want to raise children with – might never have happened.

We had a choice. And that choice protected everything we've worked so hard to build.

The truth is, many women aren't given that same freedom. Abortion restrictions fall hardest on those who already face the steepest barriers, and forced pregnancy only intensifies that injustice. These are the women most affected by systemic inequality, and forced pregnancy only intensifies that injustice.

The Secret Network Called 'Jane'

In 1969, a quiet revolution was unfolding in the backrooms of Chicago. A group of ordinary women – students, mothers, activists – began operating an underground network that they simply called *Jane*. At a time when abortion was illegal across most of the United States, women in crisis would call a secret number and hear a calm voice say, 'This is Jane. How can I help you?' What started as a referral service soon became something far bolder: when the group discovered that the man performing their procedures wasn't a doctor, they decided to learn how to do it themselves. Working in borrowed apartments with makeshift equipment, they provided safe abortions to women who had nowhere else to turn. Over four years, the women of Jane helped an estimated 11,000 women, without a single known death. In 1972, police raided one of their apartments and arrested seven members, but before the case went to trial, the Supreme Court legalised abortion nationwide with *Roe v. Wade*. Overnight, the charges were dropped, and Jane's secret service was no longer needed. What they left behind was a record of defiance and care, and a reminder of just how far women will go for one another when the system fails them.[42]

Dead people have more bodily autonomy than women

Why is the right to make decisions about our own body so controversial when it comes to abortion? The argument is often framed as 'saving a life', but that logic isn't applied anywhere else. Take organ donation, for example. There isn't a single country in the world that forces people to donate their organs, even after death, despite the fact that doing so would save lives. A dead person's bodily autonomy is still respected.

Which begs the question: why do dead people have more bodily autonomy than living women?

It's also important to understand that restricting abortion doesn't stop abortions. It stops *safe* abortions. Globally, in places where abortion is banned or restricted, women still end unwanted pregnancies, often in dangerous, life-threatening ways. Unsafe abortions account for 13% of maternal deaths globally.[43] And out of the 20 million women who go through unsafe abortions every year, 5 million will suffer long-term health complications.[44]

If you're reading this, thinking that abortions are mainly needed by reckless women who have nothing to do with you, we've got news for you: in the US and Denmark, one in four women get an abortion in their lifetime. In the UK, it's 1 in 3 women.[45–47] So if you can't think of anyone in your network who's had an abortion, it's most likely not because it didn't happen. It's likely because they didn't share it.

What about the fathers?

While two people are involved in creating a pregnancy, the burden of that pregnancy – physically, emotionally, socially and financially – falls overwhelmingly on the person who carries the child.

It's her body that undergoes the physical strain of pregnancy and childbirth. It's her health that is put at risk. It is her career, her education and her financial stability that are most often disrupted. While men can walk away (and many do), women do not have that option. As a result, 85% of single parents in the UK are mothers.[48]

That is why the decision must belong to the woman: because she is the one who faces the biggest consequences.

In total, we've had two abortions between the three of us. They both happened while on contraception, and they happened at the wrong time with the wrong partner. Today, we have three children between the three of us, with the right people and at the right time.

Motherhood has been the single most joyful experience of my life. Nothing compares to the love I feel for my son and watching him grow every day is the greatest privilege I could ask for. I'm so deeply grateful for my little family. And I am also grateful that I was able to choose when, how and with whom to embark on this journey.

That's exactly what I wish for every woman reading this chapter: the freedom and confidence to decide if you want children – and if so, to fully understand the long-term implications of your choices and shape that experience on your own terms with clarity and confidence.

THE SECRET TO SUCCESS? HAVING A PENIS

By Emma and Anna-Sophie

Women are educated like never before and working in record numbers, but that progress isn't equally reflected in positions of power. Because climbing the career ladder is still less about talent and more about privilege. The result? It's not only women who are held back, it's all of us. When half the population can't reach their full potential, organisations, economies and societies lose out too.

FACT SHEET

- There are more CEOs named Andrew and Simon than there are women CEOs among the UK's 100 largest companies.[1]
- A Spanish study found that women are 30% less likely than men to be called for a job interview when they submit an application with identical qualifications.[2]
- 76% of high-performing women receive negative feedback from their managers compared to just 2% of high-performing men.[3]
- Companies with executive teams made up of at least 30% women report net profit margins up to ten times higher than those with no women at all.[4]
- Female founders receive 2% of funding despite owning 38% of businesses and delivering 100% better returns.[5,6]

Growing up, I always assumed that the people in power had those positions because they were the most qualified. I never thought about why I mainly saw white men represented as experts in the media, as world leaders or heading companies and institutions. In fact, believe it or not, I spent years of my early adult life stating that 'I was definitely *not* a feminist', and I believed that anything was possible for those who worked hard. Needless to say, I was in for a surprise.

I remember my first real job interview. I'd worked since I was thirteen years old, taking on a variety of blue-collar jobs. But this time, I was interviewing for a student position at one of the Big Four accounting and consultancy firms. At that time, consulting was my dream job, the reason I had decided to study business in the first place, and I was buzzing with excitement to be interviewing at such a prestigious company.

I had prepared *a lot*: learning about the company, learning about the role, speaking to people in similar positions, preparing answers for the questions I expected to be asked, doing mock interviews with friends and family. I even bought new clothes for the interview, because I didn't own anything 'corporate' enough. When the day came, I felt prepared, excited and confident.

I was picked up in the lobby by two younger men, who complimented my physical appearance. I didn't think much of it as I followed them to the interview room. Here, they kicked off with questions about my motivations and academic track record. I confidently answered. A few minutes in, the questions changed character, and so did the vibe in the room. They informed me that the department I was interviewing for had no women in it, and that I should therefore expect to receive comments about my looks because I was 'a pretty girl'. My discomfort seemed to feed their confidence, and one of them asked me with a grin whether I was 'okay with that' or if I would 'go home and be sad about it'.

I felt myself resorting to the mode many women know too well: of trying to keep the peace and come across as cool, calm and collected even though it wasn't comfortable. After all, I still really wanted the job. I replied that it was 'totally okay', and 'those comments won't bother me'. 'Good,' they replied. 'Because we're not gonna change our culture just because we hire a girl.' I assured them that they wouldn't have to.

Today, I would have handled that interaction very differently. But back then, I didn't have the guts, knowledge and understanding to walk away. As I left the building after the interview, I was overwhelmed by a feeling I couldn't place. I felt embarrassed, confused and disrespected. My preparation and new outfit suddenly felt like a joke rather than a power move. Did I misunderstand something? Or did I just not fit in?

My phone was beeping with texts from friends and family asking how it went. I left them on 'read', not knowing how to answer.

It won't surprise you to hear that I didn't get the job.

That interview was my first peep into the corporate world and how it treats women. Slowly but surely, my steadfast beliefs that promotions and power were given to those who earned it began to fade. As I've progressed in my career, I've found that the misogyny and glass ceilings get worse the more you move up in the hierarchy. This discrimination doesn't only impact our careers and ambitions, it impacts our finances and opportunities in life.

We want this chapter to shine light on the challenges women still face in the workplace and what can be done to mitigate them. It's not an easy task: this is a big topic to cover in a single chapter, and there are countless books dedicated to each of these aspects. At the same time, every issue described in this chapter is significantly worse for women from marginalised communities and we could have written a whole chapter on that as well. But for now, what we want to do is connect the dots for you: to reveal the bigger picture of how these individual factors come together and compound to create an interconnected web of barriers that shape our finances and our quality of life.

The Woman Who Invented the Home Pregnancy Test

In 1967, a 26-year-old graphic designer named Margaret Crane began working at the pharmaceutical company Organon in New Jersey. Her job was simple: design packaging for cosmetics like lipsticks and creams.

One day, walking past the company's laboratory, she noticed rows of test tubes lined up over a mirrored surface. Curious, she learned that these were pregnancy tests. At the time, only doctors could administer them. A woman's urine was mixed with a chemical reagent, and after two hours, a red ring would appear at the bottom of the test tube if she was pregnant.

Margaret had a radical thought: *why couldn't women do this at home?*

With no medical background, she built a prototype for a

home test herself, naming it Predictor. Excited, she presented her idea to her boss, expecting enthusiasm. Instead, she was dismissed outright:

'If we sell this to women, we'll lose business.'

'Women won't understand how to use it.'

'This is immoral – pregnancy should only be handled by doctors.'

Undeterred, Margaret kept pushing. Eventually, Organon secretly presented her idea to their European headquarters – but without giving her credit. Months later, she heard rumours that the company was moving forward with the test. In 1969, Organon filed a patent under her name, but only if she signed away her rights for $1. She never earned anything from her invention, but agreed anyway.

In 1971, the first home pregnancy test hit the Canadian market with the slogan: *'Every woman has the right to know whether she is pregnant or not.'*

It took another five years before the test was approved in the US but by then, it was already a massive success. Within just four years of the US launch, sales of Predictor reached $40 million.[7] In 2023, the market for home pregnancy tests had reached over $700 million in the US alone.[8]

While Margaret's invention transformed the lives of millions of women worldwide, her story also highlights a familiar pattern: women's work being dismissed, stolen or left uncredited. We can't help but wonder how different the world of medicine might be today if women were better represented in positions of power.

MOST GIRLS DON'T GET THE CORNER OFFICE

If we got a penny every time we saw an average man be chosen over a brilliant woman, we'd be writing this book from a private jet.

And yet here we are.

Despite decades of progress, women are still getting paid less, promoted less, and held to different standards. Like it or not, this impacts you directly.

Globally, women earn around 77 cents for every dollar earned by men.[9] In the UK, even among full-time employees, the gender pay gap remains at 7%.[10] That's just the average. When you break it down by race, motherhood and industry, the gap widens.

Meanwhile, men dominate positions of power. In the UK, 95% of CEOs in the FTSE350 (the 350 largest, listed companies) are men.[11] In 2024, there were more CEOs named Andrew and Simon than there were women CEOs among the UK's 100 largest companies.[12] Is that because men (and people named Andrew or Simon) are better leaders, investors and founders? We've looked at the research, so you don't have to:

- **Are men better leaders?** No. Decades of research show that female leaders display more positive leadership characteristics than male leaders.[13,14]
- **Do men work harder?** No. They just (often) don't have a second job at home, doing 10+ hours of unpaid labour a week (see 'Married Men Are the Real Gold-diggers').
- **Are men better investors?** No. Research shows that women consistently achieve higher returns when investing.[15]
- **Are men better at starting and scaling companies?** No. Female founders deliver twice as much revenue per invested dollar.[16]

It's important to understand that gender bias and discrimination in the workplace isn't just bad behaviour, it's bad business. Companies with executive teams made up of more than one-third women have net profit margins ten times higher than those with no women at all.[17] The same trend is seen across industries and among companies of different sizes, when diversity is improved.

Ten. Times. Higher.[18]

With these numbers, businesses should run to solve the problem . . . right? Well, looking at the current rate of progress, the World Economic Forum estimates it will take more than 123 years to fully close the global gender gap.[19] And in recent years, the political climate has caused many companies to actively roll back diversity initiatives.

If you're feeling overwhelmed by these facts, don't worry.

We'll look at what these numbers actually mean for you. This isn't about some distant boardroom stuffed with middle-aged men named Peter. It's about the career opportunities you'll get (or won't), the salary you'll negotiate, the invisible barriers you'll hit, and the unpaid labour you'll be expected to pick up along the way. The truth is, the workplace was never designed with women in mind. It was built by men, for men, at a time when women weren't even allowed in the room. The world has changed, but the structures haven't caught up.

Here's the good news: once you see the system for what it is, you can start to play it differently. You don't have to shrink yourself, accept less, or wait patiently for change to trickle down. You can learn the rules, rewrite the ones that don't serve you, and build a career that's not only successful on paper but actually works for you.

The right person for the job

Most careers start with a recruitment process, whether that's a job interview in a swanky boardroom or a chance opportunity that turns into something more. Throughout history, there's never been a point in time where the best person always got the job. It's always been about privilege and access rather than skill and grit. Looking at the job market today, that's still the case.

The numbers back it up. Globally, women are 30% less likely than men to be called for a job interview when they submit an application with identical qualifications.[20] Why? One of the most uncomfortable truths we have to accept is this: *we're all biased.* Yes, even you. Even me. Even your super-progressive friend with pronouns in her bio and a Ruth Bader Ginsburg tote bag.

Bias isn't always about hatred, it's often about *habit.* It's the shortcut our brain takes to make quick decisions in a complex world. Unfortunately, those shortcuts are based on stereotypes, assumptions and social conditioning.

Bias against women is also seen in AI, where research shows that some systems result in significant discrimination based on both gender and race.[21] They also show that when employers review résumés, candidates with traditionally 'white-sounding' names are 50% more likely to be called back than those with names that sound African, Asian or Middle Eastern.

This happens even when the CVs are identical. One famous study shared identical résumés for a lab manager job, one with the name 'John' and the other 'Jennifer'. John was rated as more competent, more hireable, and was offered a higher salary. Same qualifications, different gender. Different outcome.[22]

The cost of gender bias in the recruitment process doesn't end with the first pay cheque, it compounds across a woman's entire career. Being passed over for opportunities, getting offered lower starting salaries or being channelled into roles with less upward mobility can add up to hundreds of thousands – sometimes millions – of dollars in lost earnings over a lifetime. That's before factoring in the missed promotions, smaller pensions and reduced financial security in retirement that follow from being undervalued at the start. In other words, every biased hiring decision isn't an isolated injustice: it's the opening chapter of a much larger story of financial inequality.

The likeability trap

If women could progress at work simply by being good at their jobs, this chapter wouldn't need to exist. But success, it turns out, doesn't look the same for men and women.

For men, ambition is a badge of honour. A man who speaks up, negotiates hard or asserts authority is praised as confident and leadership-ready. For women, the same behaviour is often seen as abrasive, bossy or difficult. This is what researchers call the 'likeability trap'. Decades of studies show that women are expected to be warm, selfless and accommodating in order to be liked. The problem is that likeability and success are negatively correlated for women. The more competent and ambitious a woman appears, the less likeable she is perceived to be.[23]

A study from Columbia Business School famously illustrated this. Two groups of participants were given the same résumé: one with the name Heidi, the other Howard. Both were equally qualified and successful. Yet Howard was seen as likeable and someone you'd want to work with. Heidi? Too self-promoting. Not a team player.[24,25]

This creates an impossible double bind: if a woman leans into ambition, she risks social push-back and professional exclusion;

if she prioritises being liked, she risks being overlooked for leadership roles, promotions and pay rises.

Data collected from performance reviews of 23,000 employees across 250 organisations shows that 76% of high-performing women received negative feedback from their managers compared to just 2% of high-performing men.[26] The same study found that men are four times more likely to be described as 'likeable'. According to Kieran Snyder, co-founder and data analyst for Textio, this has largely to do with managers' unconscious bias: women are judged more critically and on a more personal level than men. 'It's a pattern that is not often checked,' she says.[27] This likeability penalty doesn't just sting in the moment, it compounds over time and directly slows women's career progression.

You're in, now don't mess it up

Everyone makes mistakes, and failures are a normal and natural part of any career. In fact, there is a wealth of research that shows failure is an essential part of success. While men are often given the benefit of the doubt, women's errors are seen as proof of bias – often not only against the individual in question, but against women as a group. Our mistakes come with a heavier price tag. One misstep can be used to reinforce stereotypes and justify holding all women back. This is shown over and over again in research – and most people can probably recognise this from their own life.

To give an example, a study published in *JAMA Surgery* found that when a female surgeon made a mistake, she was more likely to be penalised than a male colleague. And the punishment didn't stop there: other women in the same hospital were also less likely to receive referrals after a single error made by a woman. In other words, one mistake by a woman casts doubt on all women. When a male surgeon made a mistake? Nothing happened. It was chalked up to bad luck, an outlier or an isolated case.

This double standard extends far beyond hospitals. Research from the *Harvard Business Review* has shown that women leaders are judged more harshly for failures and are more likely to be fired in the aftermath of poor company performance, even when they were not directly responsible. Men, meanwhile, are more often retained or even given second chances under the same conditions.[28]

The result? A culture where men are allowed to stumble, recover and grow, while women are punished more severely – and collectively. This stalls individual careers and reinforces the narrative that women are a 'risk' to promote or trust with authority.

It also makes it far easier for women to develop impostor syndrome. Impostor syndrome is a term used to describe the nagging sense that you don't belong, that your success is undeserved, or that one day you'll be 'found out' as a fraud. Surveys suggest that most women experience these feelings at some point in their careers,[29] which has led to the idea that impostor syndrome is an individual flaw women must fix. But here's the truth: impostor syndrome is nothing but a social construct.

What's often framed as a psychological weakness is, in reality, the by-product of biased systems. Women aren't naturally more insecure or less capable; we've been conditioned to doubt ourselves in environments where our authority is questioned, our contributions are minimised and our presence is seen as exceptional rather than normal. In other words, the problem isn't in our heads: it's in the world around us.

Labelling women with impostor syndrome conveniently shifts the burden on to us. It tells us we need to go to workshops, practise affirmations or lean in harder, instead of demanding that workplaces fix cultures that exclude, undervalue or underestimate women. The issue isn't that women feel like impostors: it's that workplaces *make us* feel like impostors.

When we stop treating impostor syndrome as a flaw in women, the narrative changes. It's not about women needing more confidence; it's about building systems that recognise our competence, normalise our leadership and make space for our ambition without questioning it. The real work lies not in 'fixing' women but in dismantling the environments that make us doubt ourselves in the first place.

On top of these double standards, women face a host of other challenges in the workplace. They're more likely to be asked to take on tasks that don't advance their careers:[30] organising the office party, mentoring junior colleagues or taking notes in meetings. These roles often go unrecognised, yet they are the invisible glue that keeps companies running. They do all of this while being met with microaggressions, biased evaluations and the constant need to prove themselves in male-dominated environments. As we explore in other chapters in this book, women also face greater interruptions in their careers due to caregiving responsibilities and health issues. We could fill an entire book with the ways women are held back. But what this amounts to, in myriad ways, is that women are promoted at far lower rates than men, despite being equally ambitious and qualified.[31]

The point is clear: career progression for women looks very different from how it does for men, and the cumulative impact over a lifetime is enormous, shaping not just opportunities, but confidence, influence and long-term financial security.

THE TRUTH ABOUT THE PAY GAP

Women get paid less in every country in the world. Yes, even when doing the same job.[32,33]

You've probably heard the excuses that 'women don't negotiate enough', that they 'choose lower-paying jobs' or that they are 'less ambitious'. But what if we're looking at this backwards: what if women aren't choosing low-paying jobs, but rather some fields are lower paid precisely because they are dominated by women?

An NYU study found that when more women move into an industry, wages drop.[34–36] There are many examples of this throughout history. When more women went into biology between 1950 and 2000 in the US, wages in biology fields fell by 18%. When women became graphic designers, wages for graphic designers fell by 34%.[37] By analyzing fifty years of data, the same study also found that and found that pay drops when professions move from predominantly male to female.[38] In short, if women do a job, it's likely to be low paid, for no other reason than that women are the ones doing it.

Why does this happen? According to Professor Paula England, 'It's not that women are always picking lesser things in terms of skill and importance. It's just that the employers are deciding to pay it less.' Her view is supported by Sam Smethers, the CEO of Surviving Economic Abuse, who states that 'This shows that it's not women's work that is undervalued, it's women'.[39]

This is not only a great example of how we undervalue women, for no reason. It's also a great example of how society often blames systemic failures on women themselves. Before anyone starts arguing that male-dominated sectors just produce more value, please ask yourself: who decides what work has value?

Of course, there are deeper, structural reasons for the gender pay gap. As discussed in the chapter on 'Money and Motherhood', having children significantly impacts women's careers, with mothers earning up to 30% less over a lifetime while fathers' wages often rise. This motherhood penalty compounds over time, showing that the pay gap isn't about individual choices, it's a systemic problem baked into the way modern work and family responsibilities are organised.

The Lean In movement

The Lean In movement started in 2013 when Sheryl Sandberg, then COO of Facebook, published the book *Lean In: Women, Work, and the Will to Lead*. It encouraged women to 'lean in' to their careers: to speak up, take risks and pursue leadership roles. The message resonated worldwide, sparking local Lean In circles in more than 150 countries, with tens of thousands of women participating in workshops, discussions and networking events.

The movement gained traction because it framed women's career advancement as something within our control. It was empowering, actionable and relatable, encouraging women to push past internal doubts and aim higher.

But the *Lean In* book and movement has faced significant criticism. Critics argue that it puts the burden of overcoming systemic barriers entirely on women, implying that if a woman struggles in her career, it's because she isn't 'leaning in' hard enough. It doesn't address structural obstacles like biased hiring, unequal pay or lack of workplace flexibility. Still, the book remains one of our generation's most cited contributions on women and work.

NEGOTIATE, NEGOTIATE, NEGOTIATE

Another common excuse for the gender pay gap is that 'women don't negotiate enough'. Research shows that this simply isn't true. A study in the *Academy of Management Discoveries* found that women actually negotiate more often than men, yet still end up with lower pay.[40] To test whether women are simply worse negotiators, USC researchers ran a series of experiments and the outcome was clear: men and women are equally good at negotiating. The difference isn't skill: it's bias. When women negotiate assertively for themselves, they are penalised (seen as aggressive or unlikeable), while men displaying the same behaviour are seen as confident and competent.[41,42] 'Women have been found to perform just as well as men when negotiating on behalf of others,' explained Professor Kim of USC's Marshall School of Business. 'It's only when they negotiate for themselves that they're penalised.'[43] Harvard Director Hannah Riley Bowles found the same: women who negotiate for higher pay are judged as less likeable, and people are less willing to work with them than with women who stay silent.

The good news is there are ways to work with the system rather than against it. Research shows that using 'relational accounts' – framing a request in a way that benefits the group or references others' support – can help women get better outcomes. For example: 'My team leader encouraged me to ask for a raise, since my compensation is low for my level' or 'We've had a strong year, and I'd love to revisit my package'. Basically: ask for what you deserve and present it as something that benefits everyone.

Frustrating? Absolutely. But if a small tweak in approach helps you get the raise or promotion, it's worth doing. Get in the room, and *then* change the rules.

Blaming the pay gap on women's negotiation skills, our lack of ambition or our career choices isn't just wrong, it's convenient. It shifts responsibility away from broken systems onto the people who are harmed by them. It tells women to 'try harder' instead of acknowledging that the rules are stacked against them. When we buy into that narrative, we're not just overlooking inequality, we're excusing it.

BEING YOUR OWN BOSS DOESN'T SOLVE THE PROBLEM

It's easy to assume that starting your own company is a way to escape workplace discrimination. After all, when you're the founder, you get to make the rules. Sadly, many women quickly learn that entrepreneurship is no escape hatch. The same gendered barriers resurface in new and brutal ways.

Nowhere is this more visible than in fundraising. For a start-up, raising capital is the fuel that allows a company to scale. Yet the odds are stacked against women, who receive just 2% of venture capital funding across Europe, the UK and the US.[44,45]

That's not a typo: nearly every dollar invested goes into male-founded companies. And yet, research consistently shows that female-founded businesses deliver better returns, generating twice as much revenue per dollar invested compared to their male counterparts.[46]

Let's repeat: female founders receive just 2% of funding despite delivering 100% better returns.

So why does the money flow to men? Part of the answer lies in investor bias – maybe because 85% of VC partners (the people who make decisions) are men.[47] In a widely cited experiment, investors were shown the exact same pitch – word for word – but delivered alternately by male and female founders. Even though the content was identical, male founders were 60% more likely to receive funding.[48] Similarly, a Harvard study found that investors pose different types of questions depending on the founder's gender: men are asked about growth and opportunity; women are asked about risk and potential losses.[49] The result? Men are set up to inspire confidence, while women are forced to defend themselves.

For us, these aren't abstract statistics or second-hand stories: they are our reality. To date, we have raised $24 million in funding. That means we're among the women in the UK who have raised the most venture capital. Ever.

Let's be clear: this is not a triumph, it's a warning sign. While $24 million is a huge sum for an individual, in the world of scaling companies it's not that crazy. For comparison, UK startups raised $16 *billion* that same year.[50] Therefore, the fact that this figure stands as a record for women is not a milestone worth celebrating, it's a reflection of how deeply stacked the system is against us.

The discrimination is not hidden. It's not subtle. It stares you down in every meeting, every pitch, every casual aside that dismisses your ambition. Over time, it wears on you. Not because you doubt yourself, or because you aren't good at what you do, but because the system keeps telling you that you don't belong.

The problem isn't only unfair to female entrepreneurs: it's costly for everyone. When capital systematically bypasses half the population, promising ideas never get the chance to scale. Jobs don't get created. Innovations don't reach the market. Economies lose out. McKinsey estimates that bridging the gender gap in entrepreneurship could add trillions to global GDP. Yet the cycle continues, not because of a lack of female ambition or ability, but because the system is designed to reward a penis over anything else.

The bottom line? Women can't simply opt out of discrimination by starting their own companies. The barriers follow them into new boardrooms, new pitches and new markets. Until we change the structures that allocate capital and define who gets to be taken seriously, the start-up world will keep wasting talent and leaving money on the table.

WHERE DO WE GO FROM HERE?

Not every woman wants the same thing from her career. Some prioritise flexibility, family or other passions over climbing the corporate ladder. Some are career-driven and want to progress. But for all of us, equal access and representation matter. Without it, talent is wasted, innovation is stifled and women's voices remain under-represented in decision-making roles. A career should be a choice, not a series of barriers stacked against you because of your gender.

So what can be done? One of the most effective tools we have is quotas. Quotas are tangible, enforceable and measurable mechanisms that give women access to positions of power. For anyone who believes quotas are wrong because 'the best person should get the job', let me be clear: I agree, and that's why we need quotas. Because right now, high-powered positions are not always filled by the most qualified people, they are filled by people with white skin and a penis. Quotas don't undermine merit; they correct decades of systemic bias and create a level playing field where women can demonstrate their abilities on equal terms. Countries and companies that adopt quotas see measurable increases in female representation, improved decision-making and healthier workplace cultures.[51–53] Quotas are not perfect, but they are the only solution so far that has consistently delivered real, measurable results.

With that said, quotas alone aren't enough. Real progress requires deep systemic change. This means educating recruiters and managers on unconscious bias, restructuring workplaces to accommodate caregiving responsibilities, implementing transparent promotion processes and redefining leadership to value collaboration and emotional intelligence alongside traditional markers of authority. It means advocating for fair parental leave policies, investment in childcare infrastructure, and pushing back against discriminatory hiring practices. True equality requires changing the structures around us, not relying on women to adapt to broken systems.

At the same time, everyday actions matter. Showing up for each other in daily life can shift workplace culture in meaningful ways. Check your own biases, give other women grace and reject the harmful narratives that pit women against one another. Supporting gender equality is a shared responsibility, from those breaking barriers at the top to those just starting out.

Equally, we need to manage our expectations of the few women who do make it to the very top, and recognise that they are already carrying an extra load– a load which is even heavier for women from marginalised backgrounds. Many women have had to work twice as hard to get there, and their very presence in those roles is already a form of resistance and representation. We cannot demand that they also shoulder the unpaid labour of being the spokesperson for every issue, mentor for every young colleague or role model in every room. Sadly, it's not uncommon to hear how women at the top are judged harshly for not living up to expectations of what they should be doing to support other women. The truth is that they might already be at capacity, working harder than any man in the same role just to *be there*. While women in powerful positions should do their part, they also need support and grace from the women around and below them.

Ultimately, all of this matters because career progression and earning potential are the foundation of financial stability. Access to career progression and equal opportunities aren't abstract ideals: they determine the resources, freedom and choices we have throughout our lives. When women are held back in their careers – whether through glass ceilings, stalled promotions or biased perceptions of leadership – the ripple effects extend far beyond the workplace. Lower earnings mean fewer opportunities to save, invest and build wealth. They translate into less bargaining power in relationships, greater vulnerability during life transitions such as divorce or career breaks and less security in retirement.

In other words, the barriers women face at work don't just close professional doors, they constrain financial independence and personal freedom. Money is not simply about numbers in a bank account, it's the tool that allows us to leave an unsafe relationship, start a business, support a child's education or retire with dignity. When systemic bias limits women's ability to earn and advance, it undermines their ability to navigate every other aspect of financial life discussed in this book.

This is why dismantling bias and creating equal opportunities isn't only a matter of fairness, it's a financial imperative. Closing these gaps gives women not just more money, but more power to shape their own lives and futures.

MENO-PAUSE: HOT FLUSH, COLD REALITY

By Anna-Sophie

Menopause shapes the second half of women's lives, yet it remains one of the most misunderstood and stigmatised transitions we face. As inevitable as puberty, it affects every woman who lives long enough. And its financial impact is very real: from medical costs to lost income and career setbacks, menopause can reshape a woman's economic future.

FACT SHEET

- 80% of women experience moderate to severe menopause symptoms.[1]
- 40% of women seeking menopause help are prescribed antidepressants.[2]
- 59% of menopausal women say their symptoms make them less able to work.[3]
- Menopause costs the UK economy 14 million working days every year.[4]
- 73% of divorced women believe that menopause contributed to their divorce.[5]

My mum is the strongest woman I know. A trained chiropractor with a PhD, she built a large successful clinic from the ground up, raised two kids, and somehow managed to be fully present through it all – never missing a school play, a music recital, a late-night phone call or a crisis. Like so many women, she carries everything without ever letting it show. She hires staff, manages a business and treats patients with the kind of care and empathy that makes people travel long distances to see her. As if that wasn't enough, she also works as a consultant for the regional health authority, where she has been responsible for developing and implementing public health programmes that improve care for people who suffer from back pain. For as long as I can remember, her work has required long hours from her. She's the kind of woman who always gets things done or takes an extra shift if needed – at work and at home.

Even though she has always worked hard, she made time for us. She would always remember everything we told her, would keep track of the family's calendar, and make each of us feel heard, seen and important. She is the kind of mother who drops everything to listen, who always shows up and who puts our needs ahead of her own. Growing up, she made it look so easy that I never realised how much it must have taken.

Ten years ago, she slowly began to change. When her menopause started, so did insomnia and brain fog. She had always been very active – playing tennis, going to the gym and running outside – but now she experienced a string of injuries and unexplained pain in various parts of her body. As a result, she spent months unable to exercise or play the sports she loved. At one point she could not even go for a walk due to a painful foot condition.

Though she had trouble sleeping, was constantly on edge and living in a body that was failing her, she still went to work, still got everything done, still showed up, never really complained. She kept going, and we kept assuming everything was okay.

Last year, she finally threw in the towel: she told us that she could not keep living like this. When she finally spoke out, I realised that the signs had been right in front of me – and I had done nothing about it. Her speaking up was the wake-up call that pushed me to act.

What I discovered next shook me even more because I found almost nothing – a medical plan, a support system, anything at all – for a condition that affects every single woman who lives long enough. Nothing for the 50% of the population living through one of the most disruptive and understudied health events of their lives.

The silence isn't just deafening – it is dangerous.

That's why we've chosen to include this chapter. Menopause doesn't only affect women physically and emotionally: it touches every corner of our lives, including our finances. It plays into and builds upon the systemic failures we explored in the 'Health is Wealth' chapter. As you'll soon see, the financial consequences of menopause can be both far-reaching and severe. It is essential knowledge for everyone, whether you're experiencing menopause yourself, approaching it or supporting someone who is. The only real way to prepare is to understand what's coming. Once you do, you'll be in a far better position to protect your health, your income and your future.

MISDIAGNOSED AND DISMISSED

Menopause happens to every person who has periods, and still we rarely hear or talk about it.

We aren't taught about it in school; doctors receive little training on it; the media barely touch it unless they're selling wrinkle cream or wellness supplements. The result? Women walk into one of the most disruptive transitions of their lives mostly unprepared.

This has consequences: 80% of women experience moderate to severe long-lasting symptoms, ranging from hot flushes and insomnia to anxiety, brain fog and joint pain.[6] These aren't mild inconveniences. They're symptoms that interfere with work, relationships and basic functioning.

Most women don't even know they're in menopause until their lives start to fall apart. They're told they're 'just stressed', 'just ageing' or 'just emotional'. And instead of hormone replacement therapy (also known as HRT) – the gold standard treatment – many are misdiagnosed with depression. In the UK, nearly 40% of women with menopausal symptoms who seek medical help are prescribed antidepressants – despite not being depressed but experiencing the wide-ranging effects of hormone imbalance.[7,8] In other words, when women turn to doctors for support during one of the biggest physical changes the human body goes through, they are too often treated as if the problem is in their minds rather than their bodies.

And to be clear, menopause is as treatable as it is real. According to gynaecologist and obstetrician Dr Dorthe Snejbjerg PhD,

HRT works by replacing the hormones that the body stops producing during menopause. This helps rebalance the body, relieves a wide range of symptoms and is effective for most women.[9] It can also offer long-term health benefits, such as protecting against osteoporosis and reducing the risk of heart disease when started early.[10,11] For many women, HRT is life-changing: they sleep better, think more clearly, feel more emotionally stable and regain energy and motivation.

Despite myths and misinformation from outdated studies, current research supports the safety and effectiveness of HRT for most women, especially when started before age sixty or within ten years of menopause.[12] It remains the most evidence-based and reliable treatment available, recommended by leading medical bodies worldwide.

In other words, it's a simple treatment with life-changing potential. Still, most women don't get offered HRT and most doctors don't push it.

I don't want to imply that this is because individual doctors don't want to help. Most likely, it's because they don't know enough about the topic: despite the fact that there are approximately 13 million menopausal women in the UK, almost half of UK medical schools do not have mandatory menopause education.[13] As a result, some doctors leave medical school with little to no education in menopause.[14] This is not a personal health issue. This is a systemic failure.

When it takes years for women to get help, the damage can be profound and permanent. Years of untreated symptoms like chronic insomnia, brain fog, anxiety and hormonal imbalance can derail careers, strain relationships and erode mental health. Confidence can wither, cognitive sharpness can fade, and some women never fully recover the version of themselves they lost while waiting for the system to take their suffering seriously.

The legacy of menopause myths

Throughout history, menopause was more than a biological change: it was stigmatised, feared and tightly controlled. In early modern Europe, menopausal women were often cast as witches, accused of disrupting social, natural and divine orders. Symptoms like hot flushes, mood swings and continued sexual activity were interpreted as signs of moral failing or even demonic influence.[15]

Medical theory reinforced these beliefs. According to ancient medical theories, menstruation expelled 'poisonous blood', keeping the body balanced. When menstruation ceased, as it does in menopause, the blood was thought to linger, making the woman's body toxic: her touch could wilt plants, spoil food or even sicken people.[16,17] This idea of older women as 'poisonous' framed them as a threat to social and familial harmony. And it wasn't a random superstition; it was part of a broader pattern of controlling women who no longer fitted the reproductive ideal.

As a result, postmenopausal women faced strict restrictions: they were advised to avoid sex, abstain from certain foods or activities, limit social interactions and refrain from anything considered indulgent or stimulating like dancing, attending the opera or pursuing intellectual interests. These prescriptions weren't medical, they were moral and social rules designed to control women.[18]

Even today, echoes of these myths persist, silently shaping how society views menopause and older women. Understanding this history reveals that menopause has always been both a natural stage and a socially constructed challenge, which poses real consequences for women's autonomy and agency.

THE SILENT CAREER KILLER

If you wanted to sabotage a woman's career just as she's reaching her peak, you couldn't design a better tool than menopause. At the exact moment many women are peaking in their careers, their bodies begin working against them.

A 2019 study found that almost 900,000 women in the UK had left their jobs because of menopausal symptoms,[19] and that 23% of women have considered resigning due to menopause.[20] According to the UK government, menopause costs the economy 14 million working days every year.[21]

This has major financial implications for individual women. Menopause often arrives when they are most experienced, most capable and statistically supposed to be earning the most. Instead, they are often forced to step back. The result? Lost income. Lost pensions. Lost leadership.

According to research by CIPD, 59% of women say their menopause symptoms make them less able to work.[22] As a consequence, many women choose to reduce hours, pass up promotions, or go part time to help cope with the symptoms and changes their body is going through. They aren't entry-level employees: they are senior leaders, policymakers, doctors, founders and teachers. They are women at the peak of their power, quietly stepping back because no one made space for them to stay. That is not a small productivity dip, it is a workforce crisis.

For many, the only solution is to scale back. Around the world, data shows that women are reducing their hours or moving into less demanding roles simply to get through this period.[23,24] These decisions aren't made lightly – they are survival tactics. The result is a shift that deeply affects women's long-term career progression and earning potential. Going part time often means lower pay, less visibility and fewer chances for promotion. The corporate ladder wasn't built for someone climbing it three days a week.

Even for those who stay full time, menopause can still put the brakes on advancement. The fatigue, the brain fog, the unpredictability: these are not small hurdles. They are the kind of challenges that make women second-guess whether they are still cut out for leadership. They are also often invisible to colleagues and bosses, which only makes it easier to overlook the women going through these challenges. This trend is often overlooked when we discuss the lack of women in leadership positions. Maybe they aren't just missing because of workplace barriers, maybe they are missing because their health forces them to step down.

The financial consequences are clear. Data shows that college-educated women see their pay growth plateau around age forty, whereas men see it increase for another decade. This is a pattern we rarely question, but it is one that mirrors the onset of menopause almost exactly. Could it be that menopause is a major, overlooked reason why women don't keep rising? Why our earning curves bend downwards, as men's keep climbing?[25,26]

This trend impacts more than monthly pay cheques: it shapes long-term financial security. The years between forty-five and fifty-five are typically peak saving years, when people put the most into pensions and investments.[27] When women step back from work, or earn less due to menopause symptoms, they contribute less. Since women already statistically live longer, earn less and are more likely to take time out for caregiving, this additional setback widens an already alarming gap.

The impact on our pensions

According to data from Fidelity, women could see their pension decrease by £18,000 if they take a one-year career break and by £36,000 if they take a two-year career break after menopause.[28] If they take a longer break to manage symptoms (e.g. five years), this could cost them £86,139 out of pocket.

It's effectively a tax on menopausal women. You can see the impact menopause symptoms could have on your pension pot if you have to take time away from work in this table below:

Time away from work	Total pension pot (8% contributions)	The cost of time away
No break	£359,380	£0
6 months' break at 51	£350,085	-£9,295
1 year break at 51	£340,985	-£18,395
2-year break at 51	£323,194	-£36,186
3-year break at 51	£305,987	-£53,393
4-year break at 51	£289,343	-£70,037
5-year break at 51	£273,241	-£86,139

Source: Fidelity International analysed ONS data on women's earnings to calculate potential impact on retirement pots, assuming a 40-year investment period (age 25–65) with 4.25% investment growth and 2% inflation. Fidelity calculated, assuming a monthly contribution of 8% in line with auto-enrolment.[29]

We've spoken before about the gender pension gap, which is observable in just about every country. Statistically speaking, the average woman retires with 70% of the income of the average man.[30] As seen in the graph below, this gap generally accelerates most dramatically after the age of 45 – just as women are more likely to work less because of menopause.[31]

Source: Broadstone's analysis of the UK Government's Office for National Statistic's Wealth and Assets Survey (December 2024). [32]

Menopause doesn't just make women *feel* worse. It makes them worse off financially too. It shortens careers, lowers lifetime income and leaves a permanent mark on pensions earnings. The poignant part is that all of this happens at the precise moment when women are most qualified, most experienced and most ready to lead.

In a world that still struggles to retain women at senior levels, this matters deeply. If we want more women in leadership, more financial equality and more balanced workplaces, we must stop treating menopause like a private problem. It is not. It is one of the most pressing professional and financial challenges women face, and it is time we addressed it like one.

OUT OF OPTIONS, OUT OF POCKET

Menopause doesn't only affect your potential earnings, it also often comes with an increase in expenses. From HRT and medical appointments to supplements, sleep aids and wellness programmes, the cost to simply feel *okay* adds up fast.

Globally, menopause is big business. In 2024, the menopause market was worth $17.79 billion, and it's projected to skyrocket to $24.4 billion by 2030.[33] That's almost equivalent to the GDP of the entire country of Armenia.[34]

The vast majority of this market? Dietary supplements. Not because they're always effective, but because in many places access to medical treatment remains frustratingly limited. When the healthcare system doesn't provide relief, many women are left to turn to whatever the wellness industry offers and to cover the costs themselves.

In the UK, HRT is available through the National Health Service. But ask any woman who's tried to get it and you'll likely hear about long waiting times, conflicting advice and constant shortages. That's assuming your GP has taken your symptoms seriously to begin with. For many women, going private is the only effective option despite steep costs: private consultations can range from £150 to £500 per appointment, with follow-ups, blood tests and prescriptions quickly running the bill higher.

Although recent reforms in the UK introduced a hormone prescription prepayment certificate (PPC), capping annual costs of the HRT medication at around £20, access still varies widely by region and GP familiarity.[35] Outside the UK, things are even patchier. In the US, for example, the annual cost for women going through menopause is estimated to be $2,100, including $400 in pharmaceutical costs.[36] In countries without strong public healthcare systems, those numbers are often out of reach, especially for women with low incomes.

Many women are therefore told to manage their symptoms through 'lifestyle changes', which often translates to a shopping list of expensive interventions: supplements, organic sleep aids, special diets, gym memberships, acupuncture, therapy, wearable tech, wellness apps and everything in between. While some of these tools can be helpful, and there isn't a one-size-fits-all programme, the cost of navigating this trial-and-error wellness maze can be high, both financially and emotionally.

Contrast this with Japan, a country often praised for how it integrates menopause care. There, treatment is more embedded in workplace healthcare, with clear guidance, medical support and culturally normalised conversations. As a result, Japanese women report fewer barriers to accessing help and more confidence in managing symptoms while staying in the workforce. The difference? A healthcare system that treats menopause like a public health issue, not a personal burden.[37,38]

Menopause is not a luxury problem. It's not a niche issue. For millions of women, the only way to keep going is to pay their way through it. This is not just unfair, it's unsustainable. When healthcare systems fail to provide adequate, affordable and stigma-free menopause care, women are pushed into private markets, where their biology becomes a business model.

Until menopause is treated with the same seriousness as any

other major health condition, women will continue to pay the price – in pounds, dollars and peace of mind.

MENOPAUSE AND DIVORCE

Right around the same time menopause strikes, another shock wave often hits women just as hard: divorce.

It's no coincidence that divorce rates spike in midlife. In fact, research shows that women between forty-five and fifty-five are at one of the highest risk periods for separation.[39] In the UK, for example, forty-five to forty-nine is the most common age range for a woman to get divorced – almost perfectly aligned with the average age of menopause.[40] While the reasons for divorce are always complex, menopause is often cited as a contributing factor, bringing physical, emotional and psychological changes that put pressure on even the most stable relationships. In fact, some studies reveal that 73% of divorced women cite menopause as a factor in their divorce.[41]

As we cover in depth in the chapter 'Married Men Are the Real Gold-diggers', the financial implications of divorce can be devastating, and midlife divorce is often far more financially destructive for women than for men. On average, women over fifty who divorce see their standard of living drop by 45%, while men experience a decline of just 21%.[42]

The consequences of this are bigger than most people realise. I remember flying home from a holiday in Australia, when I struck up a conversation with the woman sitting next to me on the plane. She explained that she worked for an Australian organisation that provides shelter for people experiencing homelessness. When I told her about my work with Female Invest, she nodded and said something that has stayed with me ever since:

in Australia, older women are the fastest-growing demographic experiencing homelessness.[43] Most of them, she explained, ended up in that situation after a relationship breakdown. Many had paused their careers to raise children or support their partners by managing the home, only to find themselves with no financial safety net when the relationship ended.

At first, I assumed this was an Australian phenomenon. Sadly, it's a trend seen in many countries around the world. In the UK, single women over fifty are among the most financially vulnerable, with rising numbers relying on social housing or support services.[44] In the US, older women face disproportionately high poverty rates after divorce or widowhood, often due to decades of unpaid caregiving and a lack of retirement savings in their own name.[45,46]

Why is midlife divorce so devastating financially? Because divorce at this stage of life doesn't only involve splitting assets. It often means losing access to shared household income, housing security, retirement funds and sometimes even health insurance. For women who paused or scaled back their careers to raise children – many of whom never fully re-entered the workforce – the financial hit is often unrecoverable.

Then come the hidden costs: lawyer fees, moving expenses, therapy, childcare, rent, and the emotional toll of navigating a major life change without a safety net, all while potentially managing severe menopausal symptoms, from insomnia to anxiety to depression. Suddenly, you're not just hot, tired and foggy: you're also single, financially unstable and starting over. That's a cruel cocktail for anyone to swallow. Yet millions of women do, often in silence.

While the world may sympathise with a woman in midlife crisis, it rarely supports her. Systems – from pensions to healthcare to tax codes – are still built around outdated norms of lifelong marriage and male breadwinners. When that model collapses, women are left footing the bill.

Menopause doesn't just impact hormones. It shakes the foundation of women's lives: from their jobs to their marriages to their futures. Unless we start connecting these dots, women will continue to pay the price in ways that are entirely preventable.

WHAT'S NEXT?

Despite everything you've just read, menopause is still not considered a protected characteristic in most employment laws. That means there's no legal requirement for employers to offer sick leave, accommodations or even basic flexibility during one of the most disruptive periods of a woman's life. No formal policies. No national strategies. In many countries, not even guidelines.

Yet the costs – personal and societal – are staggering. When experienced, capable women scale back or leave the workforce entirely, economies lose out on talent, innovation and leadership. The UK alone loses billions in GDP each year as menopausal women step back from work. But because these losses rarely show up in economic models, we don't measure them. Because we don't measure them, we don't talk about them. And because we don't talk about them, we don't fix them.

So where do we go from here?

We speak up. We ask more of our governments, our workplaces and each other. We demand national menopause strategies like the one Australia is implementing, which aims to increase training for health professionals, improve access to care, and support workplaces in improving awareness and support for employees experiencing menopause.[47,48] We ask our employers for policies, support and paid leave. Not in theory, not in vague sentiments, but in concrete practice. We push for menopause to be recognised in employment law, for training to take place in leadership teams, for flexibility to become the norm instead of the exception.

Change doesn't only happen top-down. It starts in kitchens and WhatsApp groups, in boardrooms and break rooms, with conversations between mothers and daughters, partners and friends. When we talk about menopause – *really* talk about it – we chip away at the silence that has held women back for generations. That's how stigma dies. Not with a bang, but with a million brave voices refusing to whisper.

This chapter started with my mum.

And as for her story, we took matters into our own hands. We had her hormone panels tested, along with a range of other key health markers. The results showed that she was very low in progesterone, oestradiol and testosterone. How she functioned for years at those levels is still hard for me to comprehend, let alone accept.

You'd think that finally having medical proof of such a severe hormonal imbalance would lead to immediate treatment. It didn't. She lives in Denmark – a country that prides itself on an excellent healthcare system. Yet, menopause is not on the agenda, and most GPs have little training in the topic. The number of specialists in the country could be counted on one hand, and the waiting lists were over a year long.

We looked abroad. In London, we found expensive private clinics, where the 'menopause specialists' often turned out to be general practitioners with a self-declared interest in the topic. Most clinics only had two to four medical staff. No multidisciplinary teams. No one to treat the cascade of symptoms affecting the entire body. The messaging my mum – and, I am sure, many other women facing this life-altering transition – received was often patronising at best and offensive at worst, often focused on 'fat loss injections' and 'how to get your sexy back'. For women who are struggling to function at the most basic level (with sleep, pain, anxiety, memory and energy) this kind of communication isn't just unhelpful: it's inappropriate. It reflects how poorly menopause is understood, even by those claiming to specialise in it.

After extensive searching, we did find a hormone specialist in Denmark who agreed to help. Then came the next absurd hurdle: getting our hands on the hormones my mum needed. For reasons still unclear, only a handful of pharmacies in Europe stocked the products she needed, making access difficult. It took weeks of research to track down the exact items across different countries and order them one by one. It took a huge amount of effort, time, money and privilege – but we made it work. Still, my heart aches for the women who have to navigate this without the same privilege and support system.

Over the past year, we have done everything in our power to rebuild my mum's health. This includes not only balancing her hormones, but also healing the damage done by years of being dismissed, untreated and slowly worn down. We've changed her diet, decreased her workload, started her on HRT, experimented with supplements and introduced a wide range of sleeping aids.

I am relieved to say she is doing better now. And that speaking up opened the gates for support she never imagined: colleagues who took workload from her, friends who offered emotional support and women in her network who shared similar stories and tips.

But she's still living with the aftermath of what those untreated years cost her.

I'm sharing this not only for her, but for every woman who has been left behind by a system that refuses to see her. My mother's story is not unique. It's actually fairly normal. And it shouldn't be.

When she finally opened up about her struggles with menopause, I realised just how little I knew about what my mum had been going through. It dawned on me, way too late, how many other women must be going through the same thing, quietly. If sharing her story helps even one reader feel less alone, or one woman feel more prepared, then that's the snowball effect we need.

If you're approaching menopause, or already in it, please know this: you are not alone. You deserve real medical care.

If you're someone who hasn't experienced menopause, I hope this chapter gives you the knowledge to speak up, to advocate and to check in on the women around you. Chances are, they're not okay. And trust me when I say, if you don't take action to help, you'll end up regretting it.

It's time to normalise the topic of menopause. To talk about it, track it and support the women going through it.

So I hope, as you turn the page, that you remember this not just as a chapter in a book or a series of statistics (no matter how shocking). It's a rallying cry. For awareness, for policy, for solidarity. Most of all: for every woman who deserves to thrive, not just survive, through menopause and beyond.

If you want more practical guidance and information on how to navigate menopause, we put together this free downloadable guide:

ALL THE SINGLE LADIES

By Anna-Sophie

The rise in single women isn't a rejection of love. It's a rejection of structural inequality.

FACT SHEET

- 45% of women are expected to be single by 2030.[1]
- Single women are happier than their married counterparts.[2]
- In recent years, the number of women becoming single mothers by choice has increased by 60%.[3]
- Single mothers by choice and their children are as happy as married women and their children.[4]
- Men who are dependent on their female partner's income are *five times* more likely to cheat.[5,6]

Two years ago, around Valentine's Day, we hosted an event in London about money and relationships. The goal was simple: to empower women to think strategically about their finances at different stages of a romantic relationship. We thought we had nailed it: great speakers, full room, engaged audience.

As the keynotes wrapped up and guests started mingling, a line began to form. Not to thank us, but to challenge us. Woman after woman came forward to say the same thing: *You only talked about the financial journey of a traditional, heterosexual couple.*

They were right. In trying to talk about money and love, we had defaulted to the old narrative. One that assumes every woman will fall in love, move in, get married and build her financial life around a romantic partner. And that's not the world we live in anymore.

Today, more women than ever are choosing to stay single, to create chosen families, to build wealth on their own terms, to build relationships that don't follow conventional timelines – or don't include men at all. Our community called us out. They were right to. We had fallen into the very stereotype we exist to challenge: the idea that a woman's financial life revolves around a man.

We left that night humbled and more committed than ever to broadening the conversation. Money and relationships aren't one-size-fits-all, and women deserve advice that reflects the full spectrum of their choices.

The feedback from our members is ultimately what inspired this chapter. The rise of single women is not only a cultural shift, it's an economic one too. For the first time in history, women are no longer forced into relationships for survival. We can earn our own money, live on our own terms, and decide for ourselves what a successful life looks like. When given that choice, many women are walking away from the traditional script entirely.

This shift has massive financial implications. It changes how we earn, how we spend, how we invest and how we build our futures. It's reshaping the economy in ways the world is only just beginning to understand. Before anyone tells you this is about loneliness or failure, let's look at what's really happening, and why single women might just be rewriting the rules of success.

45% OF WOMEN WILL SOON BE SINGLE

We are living through a historic moment: more women than ever are choosing to build lives without marriage – or at least, on their own timeline. In the US, a record 52% of women were unmarried in 2021, a drastic shift from just 7% in 1900.[7] Across Europe and Asia, similar trends are playing out: women are delaying marriage and prioritising education, autonomy and career growth.

As a result, nearly half of women in the UK, US and other developed countries are expected to be single by 2030.[8] This might sound like a crisis, at least according to traditional narratives that still idealise marriage as the ultimate female aspiration. But look a little closer and this shift reveals something far more exciting: single women are thriving.

Data consistently shows that single women are happier, healthier and wealthier than their married counterparts.[9] A growing body of research also shows that single women tend to have better mental health, lower levels of stress and more fulfilling social lives. They are more likely to exercise regularly, sleep better and invest more in their personal growth and professional development. They're thriving not *in spite* of being single, but *because* of it.

The same cannot be said for men. And the correlation is pretty clear: historically, women have been expected to sacrifice their dreams, finances, health and happiness to support those same areas for their husband. What did they get in return? Limited freedom, unequal pay and a second shift of unpaid labour at home. When women choose to opt out of that arrangement, every area of their life improves while the opposite is said for men, who lose access to the unpaid labour of a wife: her emotional labour, her domestic work, her role as his unofficial therapist and life organiser. We look at the implications of this in more detail in 'Masculinity Meltdown'.

As we discuss in 'Married Men Are the Real Gold-diggers', marriage as a concept was originally never about love. It was a system designed to control women: economically, socially, sexually. In many parts of the world, that is still the case today, but the rise of single women is challenging that legacy.

Single women are driving consumer spending, reshaping housing markets and creating new models of community. They are choosing freedom, autonomy and ambition over outdated expectations. In doing so, they're not only transforming their own lives, they're reshaping the world around them.

In the past decade, the number of single, unmarried women in the workforce has grown three times faster than the overall pool of workers.[10] As women accumulate degrees (we now graduate from university at higher rates than men[11]) and join the labour force in record numbers, we're reshaping GDP and consumer culture. In the US alone, women contribute an estimated $7 trillion annually to GDP, with single women outspending average households across apparel, beauty, dining and travel.[12]

This phenomenon (sometimes called the 'She-conomy') is truly global. Women now account for 70–80% of all consumer purchasing decisions, influencing industries from home-buying to wellness to tech innovation.[13] And single women are not only consumers, they're business founders, investors and innovators. Interestingly, whenever data on women spending money emerges, they are portrayed as frivolous spenders, spending men's hard-earned money. So this is your reminder: women make and spend their own money.[14] In fact, unmarried, childless women in the US earn 8% more than single men. This is known as 'the reverse pay gap' and it's often attributed to the fact that single women have higher levels of education than the average single man.[15,16]

Financially, single women are doing well. Unmarried women are closing the gender wealth gap faster than married women. In the US, single women under thirty now out-earn their male peers in major cities like New York, Los Angeles and Washington, DC.[17] They're also buying homes at higher rates: in 2021, single women accounted for nearly 20% of all home purchases – nearly double the rate of single men.[18] This matters, because home ownership has long been a gateway to financial security and wealth accumulation.

Freedom from the traditional roles of wife and mother often means women have more time, energy and resources to invest in their careers, communities, passions and friendships. They're more likely to pursue higher education, travel, start businesses or support causes they care about. Their economic footprint is expanding: in countries across Europe, Asia and North America, single women are becoming a powerful consumer bloc – one that is independent, values-driven and less tied to family-centred purchasing patterns.

The cost of being single

Even though the decision to stay single can be an act of empowerment, it often comes with a financial penalty. Single people face what's known as the 'singles tax': the hidden financial cost of living alone. Without a partner to share household expenses, rent or mortgage payments, single people shoulder a disproportionately high cost of living. They're also penalised in certain areas of tax systems, which often assume a dual-income household as the norm. Over time, these disadvantages compound to reduced savings, reduced investment opportunities and reduced long-term financial security.

There's also an emotional burden to being single, especially when it comes to finances. While the freedom to make your own financial decisions can be empowering, it also means carrying the full weight of financial responsibility. There's no partner to split bills with, no second income to fall back on, and no one to share the stress when unexpected expenses hit. If you lose your job, there's no built-in safety net. If you take a financial risk, you bear the consequences entirely. For many single women, that double-edged sword – being both totally free and totally responsible – can feel like an added pressure.

When we talk about the financial downsides of being single, there's a critical distinction between being *single by choice* and *single not by choice*. Nowhere is that more evident than in the financial fallout of divorce. As we explore in more detail in 'Married Men are the Real Gold-diggers', after a split, women's household income drops by an average of 41%, compared to just

23% for men. While some eventually recover, many don't. This is especially true for mothers who gave up full-time work to care for children or support their partner's career. Women who end up as single mothers not by choice are often among the most vulnerable groups in society.

In the UK, nearly 71% of single-parent households were deemed financially fragile, with few emergency savings and higher reliance on borrowing. For context, the vast majority of single-parent households are led by women. On the individual level, in 2019 single women with dependent children in the US had a median net worth of just $7,000 compared to $65,000 for single women without children.[19]

Who is better off?

So who's better off financially: single women or married women?

It's hard to generalise, and the answer to this will also vary by country. If we had to make an overall claim, however, research increasingly suggests that being single can be the better long-term financial decision for many women, despite the single tax and the financial burdens of living on one income. And that's because the real cost isn't rent or utilities: it's the cumulative financial toll of traditional partnership roles.

A comprehensive study from Japan showed that when measuring personal net worth (wealth held solely in a woman's own name), never-married women consistently have higher net worth than their married counterparts, especially among younger and middle-aged groups.[20] This difference is largely driven by the fact that single women are more likely to work full time and sustain continuous career growth, while married women frequently face labour market disruptions related to marriage and childbearing.

When looking at *household* wealth, married women may

appear wealthier. However, this is only under the assumption that spouses share assets equally, which often doesn't reflect reality. In fact, married women's personal ownership of assets is often limited, and the unequal sharing of wealth within marriage means that their economic independence and financial security can be significantly constrained.[21]

All of which shows that, while singlehood may seem costly up front, a lifetime of trade-offs within a traditional marriage can end up costing far more: in money, and in control, independence and dignity.

DO WOMEN (AND MEN) STILL WANT RELATIONSHIPS?

Does the rise of single women mean that women no longer want relationships? The answer is pretty simple: no.

A 2022 Pew Research Center study found that single women are split pretty much down the middle when it comes to this question, and around 50% of single women are still looking to date.[22] But here's the catch: we're no longer willing to settle. What today's women want isn't a fairy tale or a financial provider, it's a partnership. And that's where the disconnect begins.

Plenty of men want partnership, too, and after generations cast as sole providers, many are figuring out who they are in an equal partnership. That doesn't call for lower standards; it calls for better partnerships built on reciprocity. Today's women are better educated and more financially independent than ever. They won't sign up to be an unpaid housekeeper, emotional manager or career support system. They want an equal, so when that's rare, they choose to stay single.

But instead of celebrating single women raising the bar, society often villainises them. We tell them they're being too picky, unrealistic, or that they'll 'regret it later'. But here's the uncomfortable truth: if these women are already meeting the standards they expect in a partner – emotional maturity, financial stability, ambition – then maybe the problem isn't their expectations. It is that too many men are still comfortable offering less.

This is not about bashing men. It's about recognising that the institution of heterosexual relationships has long been structured to benefit one side more than the other. As more women wake up to that imbalance, they're choosing to opt out until the terms improve.

The 4B movement

The 4B Movement started in South Korea as a bold act of rebellion against a society where women were expected to marry young, have children, and sacrifice their careers to fit a mould designed for them. 4B stands for the 'Four Nos': no dating, no sex with men, no marriage and no childbirth. On the surface, it might sound extreme, but at its heart, 4B is about rejecting the rules of a game that was rigged from the start. For many South Korean women, choosing 4B became a way to reclaim their lives, their money and their futures, free from patriarchal expectations that left them exhausted and undervalued. Today, the movement has grown across borders, inspiring women across the world, in the US and beyond. What 4B proved is that sometimes the most powerful way to demand change is not by asking politely, but by walking away from systems that no longer serve you.

On the flipside, even though some men complain about women's 'unrealistic standards', many still hold on to outdated expectations themselves, particularly when it comes to power and money. Research shows that men in heterosexual relationships often prefer to earn more than their partners.[23] And when they don't, the impact goes far beyond pride: men who are not the primary earners are significantly less trusting of their partner's spending and investing decisions, and over half say that the financial dynamic creates tension in their relationship.[24] Men report higher life satisfaction when they out-earn their wives, and significantly lower satisfaction when their partner earns more.[25]

According to a study published in *American Sociological Review*, men who make less money than their female partner are also significantly more likely to cheat. Men financially dependent on their partners were, in one study, up to five times more likely to cheat.[26,27] The researchers claim this may be a result of men feeling threatened and cheating provides a way for them to reassert their 'masculine identity'.

THE RISE OF SINGLE MOTHERS BY CHOICE

One of the most liberating outcomes of women's growing financial independence is the ability to make choices that once felt impossible, including the choice not to settle. This shift is reflected in two powerful trends: one, global birth rates are falling, as more women opt out of traditional paths to motherhood. In the past fifty years, global birth rates have decreased by 50%.[28,29]

And two: among those who want children, increasing numbers are choosing to become single mothers by choice. In recent years, the number of women becoming single mothers by choice has increased by 60%, according to the European Sperm Bank.[30]

With the increasing accessibility of fertility treatments, egg freezing and donor options, women are more empowered than ever to become parents without waiting for a suitable partner – or settling for an unsuitable one.

Of course, being a single parent comes with financial realities that differ from those faced by partnered parents. The upfront costs alone are significant. Fertility treatments such as IVF, commonly used by women pursuing solo motherhood, cost around $21,600 on average per cycle in the US,[31] with many women requiring multiple cycles to achieve a successful pregnancy. Additionally, expenses such as medications, sperm donation and legal fees add to the financial burden. For those who opt for adoption, costs can range from $5,000 to $40,000, depending on where they live and the route chosen.[32] These initial investments are substantial, but they represent only the beginning of the financial journey for single mothers by choice. For many, these routes remain financially out of reach. If we are to be serious about autonomy, we need to make fertility care more accessible through transparent pricing, public support and fair coverage.

Childcare is another major financial challenge. Without a co-parent to share responsibilities or costs, solo mothers bear the full weight of childcare expenses. In the UK, the average annual cost of raising a child under eighteen years is £12,500, according to *The Times*.[33] On top of that, if we go back to the single tax we described earlier, this is felt more keenly once children are involved. Solo mothers often experience fewer savings, greater reliance on borrowing and increased vulnerability to financial shocks.

It's easy to look at the numbers and conclude that being a single mother by choice is more expensive. After all, there's no one to split the cost of fertility treatment, nappies or nursery fees. You pay the full price for everything: childcare, rent, school uniforms. On paper, yes, the financial burden is heavier. But over time, it's not *necessarily* more expensive.

Most of us have watched friends have children with partners who hold them back. Men who don't pull their weight at home, who leave them to carry the vast majority of the emotional load, the logistics, the school drop-offs and dentist appointments. Men who also don't contribute equally financially yet expect to be treated as equals. I've seen how these women begin to deprioritise their own careers, not because they want to, but because they have no other choice. That's not a season: it's a life path redirected.

That's a cost you carry for decades. The missed promotions. The smaller pension pot. The part-time roles taken to keep the household afloat. The dreams that get filed away under 'maybe later'. It's heartbreaking to watch, and I've seen it more than once. Suddenly, the cost of childcare and nappies seems insignificant next to a lifetime of financial and emotional loss because of the wrong partner.

Yes, single motherhood by choice comes with a clear and visible price tag. But choosing the *wrong* partner – one who drains you financially, emotionally and professionally – comes with a hidden cost that lasts a lifetime. And if we're being honest, we've all seen too many women settling for a partner like this.

This is not about rejecting love or relationships: it's about rejecting the idea that motherhood must come with a man attached. For generations, women were pressured into marriage for financial stability and cultural pressure. For example, it wasn't until 1975 that British women could open a bank account or apply for a mortgage without a man's permission.[34] That story is being rewritten. And here's the part that matters most: it's working.

Research from the *European Journal of Developmental Psychology* shows that children of single mothers by choice do just as well emotionally and socially as those with two parents.[35] In fact, some studies suggest they may experience *less* conflict and emotional distress at home.[36] A study from Cambridge University echoes this and adds that parenting stress levels in single-mother-by-choice households were lower than in two-parent families where relationship conflict existed. According to the study: '*The findings suggest that the presence of two parents – or of a male parent – is not essential for children to flourish.*'[37]

One more time: having two parents or a male parent is not essential for children to flourish. Let's all pause and make sure this sinks in.

The study continues: '*This adds to the growing body of evidence that family structure is less influential in children's adjustment than the quality of family relationships.*'[38]

No one is saying that being a single mother is better than being a mother with a good partner. But we are saying that being a single mother is better than being with a bad partner – and research backs us up.

For too long, the cultural script told women to find 'a man, *any* man' in order to start a family. What if that man brings instability, resentment or zero shared responsibilities? That's not a partnership. That's a burden.

To anyone offended by this trend, ask yourself this: why do you want women to sacrifice their health, happiness and finances just so a man (who maybe doesn't even contribute equally to the work that comes with having a child) can call himself a father?

Single mothers by choice are not broken families. They are *intentional* families. They are proof that women are no longer waiting for permission (or for perfect circumstances) to build the lives they want. They are choosing motherhood not because they have to, but because they *want* to.

And that, frankly, is something worth celebrating.

HOW TO FLOURISH FINANCIALLY AS A SINGLE WOMAN

Being single can be deeply empowering. You get to make your own decisions, define success on your own terms, and live life unapologetically in alignment with your values. It also comes with unique financial considerations, because there's no one else to fall back on, no partner to split the bills with, no joint retirement plan, no built-in safety net. Even though many single women have strong communities of friends, family and trusted people they've intentionally chosen to be in their life, there's no automatic fallback. That's both scary and liberating.

It means you have full control, but also full responsibility. That's why single women need to think about money differently. Whether you're single by choice or by circumstance, it's essential to take proactive steps to build a financial life rooted in independence, clarity and long-term security. You're not just building wealth: you're building a life where you have your own back, every step of the way.

To flourish financially, the first step is to build protection around yourself. That means making smart choices about health insurance, life insurance, retirement planning and emergency funds. It means understanding your credit score, setting intentional financial goals and creating a life plan that supports the future you want.

Of course, the standard financial advice still applies: pay off high-interest debt, diversify your investments and have a budget that works for you (ideally automated and focused on spending in alignment with your values). You can dive deeper into all of this inside the Female Invest app.

In the following pages, we've gathered some of the most important financial steps to take, designed to help you thrive on your own terms.

Become financially literate

The first step is to take time to build financial literacy. Understanding the basics of money (like budgeting, saving, investing, credit and debt) gives you the confidence to make smart decisions and avoid costly mistakes. Financial literacy isn't about knowing everything overnight; it's about building knowledge step by step so you feel empowered rather than overwhelmed.

Focus on topics relevant to your current situation, like improving your credit score or understanding retirement accounts. The more you know, the easier it becomes to set realistic goals and choose the right financial products. And trust us: learning about money doesn't have to be difficult.

Pro tip: If you need personalised guidance and access to experts, Female Invest has built a world-leading education app to help you, no matter where you're from or where you start.

Set financial goals

Having a clear vision for your future helps turn your financial dreams into achievable steps. Whether you want to buy a home, start investing, travel or build a retirement nest egg, defining specific goals gives your money purpose and direction.

Break your life plan into short-, medium- and long-term goals. For example, short-term could be saving for a vacation, medium-term might be building a down payment for a home and long-term could be retirement savings. Assign timelines and dollar amounts to each goal to make them concrete.

Pro tip: Make sure you automate savings towards these goals, so your money works for you consistently without you having to think about it each month.

Build a solid emergency fund

A solid emergency fund is your financial shock absorber. It gives you breathing room when life throws you a curveball – whether it's job loss, medical expenses, a family crisis or even a global pandemic.

Your emergency fund should have enough to cover at least three to six months of essential living expenses (rent, bills, food, transport). If your income is irregular or you're self-employed, consider saving closer to nine to twelve months for extra peace of mind.

This money needs to be readily available for when an emergency occurs, and therefore you can't invest it. Instead, keep it in a separate high-yield savings account. In that way, you still get a return on the money while keeping it readily available.

Pro tip: The easiest way to make sure you prioritise your emergency fund is to automatise a monthly transfer into it – even if it's just a small amount. Consistency matters more than size.

Prepare early for retirement

Retirement might feel far away, but the earlier you start saving, the more time your money has to grow through compounding. Experts often recommend aiming to replace about 70–80% of your pre-retirement income to maintain your lifestyle once you stop working. To estimate how much you need, multiply your expected annual expenses by the number of years you anticipate being retired (often twenty to thirty years).

Start by contributing at least 10–15% of your income to retirement savings, adjusting as you get older or your financial situation changes. Use tax-advantaged accounts where possible and diversify your investments across stocks, bonds and other assets to balance growth and risk (again, if you're unsure, you can learn how to do this in the Female Invest app). Review your retirement plan annually to keep it aligned with your goals and life changes.

Pro tip: Use retirement calculators to set personalised savings goals and schedule automatic contributions.

Understand and protect your credit score

Your credit score is the key that unlocks access to better financial opportunities like lower interest rates, higher credit limits, and even approval for renting a home. A strong score signals that you're trustworthy with money, while a low score can make life more expensive.

The biggest factors affecting your score are paying bills on time, keeping credit card balances low (ideally under 30% of your limit) and maintaining a long credit history. Avoid applying for too much credit at once, as each application can temporarily lower your score.

Check your credit card statement regularly to catch errors or fraud early, and set up reminders or auto-pay to make sure you never miss a due date on repayments.

Pro tip: If you're just starting to build credit, consider a low-limit credit card or a secured card – and treat it like a debit card by paying it off in full each month. It builds your score without building debt.

Get life insurance

If anyone depends on your income (like children, siblings or ageing parents), life insurance isn't optional: it's a vital safety net that ensures your loved ones are financially protected if something happens to you.

Start with a term life insurance policy that covers your working years and provides enough to pay for childcare, housing, education and daily expenses. Even if you don't have children, life insurance can help cover funeral costs or debts so no one else is left to pay.

What to look for:

- ✓ A payout that reflects your dependants' needs
- ✓ Fixed premiums over the policy term
- ✓ A reputable insurer with good claims history
- ✓ Clearly named beneficiaries

What to avoid:

- ✗ Overpaying for whole life or bundled products you don't need
- ✗ Choosing a payout that's too low
- ✗ Forgetting to update your policy as life changes

Pro tip: Review your life insurance policy annually or after major life changes (like having a child, changing jobs or buying a home) to make sure your coverage still fits your needs.

Get health insurance

If you're single, and especially if you're self-employed or free-lancing, having good health insurance is essential. It protects you from costly medical bills and income loss if you get sick or injured. As we discuss in the chapter on 'Health is Wealth', women statistically spend more years sick and are more likely to seek costly private care. Don't rely on luck or the hope that nothing will happen.

What to look for:

- ✓ Comprehensive coverage including (private) doctor visits, prescriptions, emergency care and preventive services
- ✓ Low out-of-pocket maximums to limit your annual expenses
- ✓ A wide network that includes your preferred doctors and hospitals
- ✓ Disability or income protection benefits if you can't work due to illness or injury

What to avoid:

- ✗ Plans with high deductibles but limited coverage that leave you exposed to big bills
- ✗ Hidden fees, confusing exclusions, or waiting periods that reduce your coverage
- ✗ Narrow provider networks forcing you to switch doctors or pay more out-of-pocket
- ✗ Bundled add-ons that increase premiums without real value

Pro tip: If your job doesn't offer health benefits, consider joining a professional association or cooperative that offers group health insurance plans. They often have better rates and coverage than individual plans.

THIS IS JUST THE BEGINNING

The rise of single women is an exciting time, full of possibilities. As more women choose themselves – whether for a season or for a lifetime – they are rewriting the narrative of what a fulfilled, successful life looks like.

This shift has the power to transform everything. Cities and policymakers are starting to catch up: in Belgium, a local council passed a 'singleton charter' to ensure that laws, housing, events and outreach efforts account for the needs of single adults.[39] Businesses are shifting their strategies too, speaking directly to women who travel solo, invest independently and buy with confidence.

As traditional family structures evolve, so too does the definition of home. More and more women are choosing to live together in alternative community set-ups, whether it's single mothers supporting each other under the same roof, best friends co-owning property or multigenerational households led by women. These new forms of living are not only practical, they're empowering. By pooling resources, sharing childcare and creating emotional support systems, women are building communities that offer both freedom and security. It's a quiet revolution that challenges the outdated idea that a family must consist of a mother, father and children to function or thrive. The truth is: a family is whatever you choose to make it.

For this movement to be truly liberating, systemic change

must follow. We need to close the gender pay gap, stop penalising single-income households and reform financial systems that still assume marriage as the default. Women don't just deserve stories of empowerment, they deserve actual autonomy, support and security.

When we recently shared content about the rise of single women on our platforms, the response was overwhelming. Women of all ages, backgrounds and life stages reached out to tell us that becoming single had been one of the most liberating and fulfilling chapters of their lives.

One woman in her early forties wrote, '*I used to think something was wrong with me because I hadn't settled down. But now I see my independence as my biggest asset. I've built a life that's truly mine.*'

Others told us about the joy of buying their first home solo, travelling the world without compromise or simply waking up every day free from expectations that never quite fitted them. These messages didn't come from a niche group: they came from teachers, entrepreneurs, students, mothers and retirees.

In many ways, this chapter is a tribute to our members. Thank you for putting this topic on the agenda, for challenging us, for inspiring us and for constantly pushing us to evolve. You are the reason we do this work.

MASCU-LINITY MELTDOWN

By Anna-Sophie, Camilla and Emma

When you are used to privilege, equality feels like oppression. And that's exactly what we're seeing today, as men are falling behind in the very system they built themselves. The result? A masculinity meltdown.

FACT SHEET

- Boys lag behind girls at all levels of education in the UK, US and Europe.[1–4]
- The percentage of unemployed UK men has doubled since 1970.[5]
- 28% of US men under thirty have no close social connections.[6]
- 56% of UK men think that feminism has gone too far.[7]
- Since 2018, there's been a 500% increase in young UK men attending church.[8]

We spent a good amount of time debating whether or not to include this final chapter. The purpose of this book is to centre women, to focus on *our* reality and how we might navigate a (financial) world that wasn't built for us. So what place does a chapter about men have in a book like this? At first, the idea felt contradictory.

But as we sat with the question, the answer became unavoidable: we cannot talk honestly about building equality without talking about men. To leave them out entirely would be to ignore one of the most stubborn and powerful forces shaping women's financial lives: the patriarchy, and the way it distorts not only women's opportunities, but men's identities too. If we are serious about dismantling the barriers holding women back, then we must also be serious in asking what role men play in sustaining these barriers, and what role they *must* play in tearing them down.

To be clear, this is not about vilifying men. As we said in the Introduction to the book, our aim isn't to be anti-men. It never was. The purpose of this chapter is not to bring men down, but to challenge them to rise higher. Equality cannot be built on one-sided effort. It cannot rest solely on women bending, twisting and contorting ourselves to survive. It must also involve men doing the work: interrogating the ways toxic masculinity has limited them, and then choosing differently. That work is uncomfortable. It is demanding. It asks more of men – more humility, more courage, more accountability – than they have historically been asked to give. It is also necessary.

Because for too long, society has excused, coddled, lowered expectations and rewarded mediocrity for men, while women have been told we need to over-perform just to get a seat at the table. We believe men can do better. We believe the men we love – our partners, brothers, fathers, friends – are capable of rising to the challenge of a truly equal world, but only if we hold them to a higher standard than they've been held to before. This is especially important at a time where 56% of UK men believe that 'equality has gone too far'.[9]

So this chapter exists because equality is not a women's project alone. It's a collective one, and part of that collective work is calling men in and asking them to shoulder their share of the burden. To fight against toxic masculinity not just for women's sake, but for their own. To stop being part of the problem and start being part of the solution.

This is the hope that runs through these pages: not that men must lose so women can win, but that when men do the hard work of unlearning, confronting and changing – everyone gains.

THE MASCULINITY CRISIS

There is no denying that masculinity is in crisis. Boys are falling behind in school. Men are facing a mental health epidemic with higher rates of suicide than women. Male loneliness is reaching historic levels, with men reporting fewer friendships and more difficulty forming romantic relationships. These are not trivial issues. They shape lives, families and entire societies, and they demand thoughtful solutions.

Some of these challenges are made worse by larger economic shifts. The decline of industrial jobs, the rise of automation and globalisation have left many men without the steady work that once defined their role and identity. For generations, men were told their value lay in providing, and when those anchors vanish, it is not surprising that many feel destabilised.

Yet contrary to the claims made by conservative voices, these struggles are not caused by women. Feminism is not what is making men falter. In fact, research by the American Psychological Association points to rigid gender norms – not feminism – as a root cause of men's mental health struggles. When men are raised to see vulnerability as weakness and emotion as shameful, a lost job or a failed relationship becomes not just a setback but a crisis of identity.

Still, the masculinity crisis is often framed as if boys and men are passive victims, with an expectation placed on women to solve their problems. This is especially seen in the rising popularity of the 'manosphere', where the central claim is that feminism is harming boys and men. But blaming women stops us from examining the true cause: the suffocating script of traditional masculinity itself.

The bottom line: boys and men are facing a crisis. A crisis born not of women gaining rights, but of a narrow, outdated idea of what it means to be a 'real man'. Until we confront that truth, we won't find real solutions.

When you're used to privilege, equality feels like oppression

Ironically, the masculinity crisis is driving men deeper into the very thing that created the crisis to begin with: toxic masculinity. As traditional male dominance erodes, we're seeing a dangerous backlash in the form of rising conservatism, the 'manosphere' and a renewed popularity of 'Christian' values among men. This is especially visible among young people, where Gen Z men are more religious than their female peers.[10] Instead of addressing the real roots of their struggles, many retreat into reactionary ideologies often with subtle and not-so-subtle misogynistic tenets, which promise to restore the power and importance they feel slipping away.

Research shows a generational split: young women are moving sharply to the political left, while young men are drifting to the right, fuelled by influencers pushing the language of 'red pills' and 'blue pills'. These online communities glorify outdated gender hierarchies, demonise women and present submission as women's natural role. The growth of these spaces isn't a coincidence. It's a symptom of men clinging to the very structures they once controlled but are now failing to thrive within. Truth is twisted, misinformation becomes a shield against accountability and grievance is sold as identity.

Terrible? Absolutely. Surprising? Not really. Social media platforms, largely built and shaped by men (often white and in positions of unchecked power), have become amplifiers of hate. Opinions and beliefs are no longer formed in the family home, guided by parents and caregivers, but on phones and screens where young people encounter unmoderated content.[11] On average, it takes less than thirty minutes from a young man setting up an account on Instagram, TikTok or YouTube before he is recommended misogynistic content.[12] All of this manufactures isolation: the more grievance a man consumes, the harder it becomes to form the mutual, respectful relationships that actually protect against loneliness.

This might help explain why more men than ever are single. Put bluntly: women are not interested in dating men who hate them. And ironically, the rise of single men poses a danger not just to women but to society as a whole. On average, single men are over-represented in statistics on violence, radicalisation, racism, homophobia and belief in conspiracy theories.[13–19] In other words, the men most resistant to change are also those most likely to destabilise society. Rather than recognising that the unpaid labour of women has long been the invisible scaffolding of their lives, they lash out at women's independence, blaming feminism instead of acknowledging their own dependence on work they never valued.

Perhaps the most striking trend is the growing popularity of Christianity among men. To be clear, faith itself is not the problem. Religion can offer belonging, meaning and stability, especially in a time of loneliness. It's not surprising either that in times of global instability, or during seismic shifts like climate change and the rise of AI, many turn to religion as a way to find certainty in an uncertain world. But in too many conservative churches, this revival is tied to a regressive promise of 'traditional family values' and a return to 'natural order'. At the heart of this narrative is a toxic script: women must submit, men must lead, and any deviation from this model is treated as a moral failure. For men struggling to find identity in a system that no longer guarantees them success, controlling women becomes a shortcut to feeling powerful again.

What we're witnessing is not a cultural renaissance but a regressive retreat. Instead of confronting the flaws of traditional masculinity and embracing equality, too many men are doubling down on ideologies that harm not only women, but also themselves.

THE MALE LONELINESS EPIDEMIC

For the first time in history, women aren't being forced into marriage for financial survival or social legitimacy. Just fifty years ago, a woman in the UK couldn't even open a bank account in her own name without her husband's permission. Today, women are earning their own money, building their own careers and, crucially, making their own decisions about the kind of life they want to live.

That freedom of choice is revolutionary. When women are no longer economically or socially dependent on men, they are free to walk away from relationships that drag them down. And increasingly, they are. This doesn't mean women are giving up on love; it means they're giving up on unequal partnerships. When the choice is between being single and being with someone who cannot meet them as an equal, more and more women are choosing themselves.

This shift, while liberating for women, has left many men unmoored. For generations, men could assume access to women's unpaid labour – the personal assistant, the therapist, the housekeeper, the caregiver, all rolled into one. When that quiet scaffolding falls away, many men find themselves struggling to adjust.

The result is what researchers now call a male loneliness epidemic. In the US, for example, 28% of men report having no close connections,[20] and men in general are twice as likely as women to have no one to go to for emotional support.[21] For many, a romantic partner has become their only source of intimacy and care, so when that relationship ends or never forms, the isolation can feel crushing. It is heartbreaking, but it is also predictable: too few men have been encouraged to build and sustain meaningful relationships outside of romance, or to see emotional openness as a strength.

And yet when women choose to opt out, when we decide we'd rather be alone than in draining, one-sided partnerships, the conversation so often shifts to panic about men's pain rather than recognition of women's progress. Suddenly, it's an 'epidemic'. Women are told to lower our standards, to settle for less, to keep giving chances, to bend ourselves into the kind of partner who makes life easier for someone else. Why? So that no man has to face being alone.

So when people ask *Where have all the good women gone?*, we can't help but respond: *Are you really surprised?* After generations of treating women as caretakers first and individuals second, of building systems that worked for most men but not for most women, what exactly did you expect?

We are finished being the unpaid labourers of society. Finished with the expectation that we should give up our dreams, bodies, careers and identities in exchange for so little – and still feel grateful and look pretty while doing it.

If society genuinely cared about women, it would be building a world that supports us: a world with affordable childcare, equal domestic responsibility, healthcare that takes women seriously. A culture that doesn't punish us for being ambitious or independent. Instead, when we step back and say 'no thank you', we're called selfish. Picky. Unreasonable.

So perhaps the problem isn't that women are raising our standards. Perhaps the problem is that too many men have stopped rising to meet them. This isn't about women rejecting men, it's about refusing to lose ourselves, to sacrifice our futures, or to bankrupt our finances and our mental health for relationships that don't give us what we deserve.

And honestly? Good for us. We do deserve better.

VIOLENCE AGAINST WOMEN

Trigger warning: *The next sections contain themes of sexual assault, violence and abuse, which some individuals may find distressing. Please skip to page 178 if you want to avoid reading these sections.*

The crisis that masculinity is quickly spiralling into – and the rage many men feel from failing in a system that has historically supported them – has tragic repercussions for women. Because this male anger and frustration is being channelled into hate and misogyny, fuelling a culture of (sexual) violence.[22] While this is one of the most difficult and painful parts of women's story, we cannot leave it out. Finance might look like numbers, choices and opportunities, but for millions of women, money is also tied to safety, freedom and survival. To ignore that would be to tell only half the truth.

This is not an easy chapter to read, nor was it to write. Normally, we aim to make conversations about money empowering, even fun. But some realities are too heavy to sugarcoat, and violence against women is one of them. So please, read the next few sections with kindness, and courage.

As any woman will know, sexual violence is an integral part of our experience. It plays out in so many big and small ways: the lingering looks from grown men when we hit puberty, the fear of walking alone at night, the unwanted touches in public spaces, the sex we feel pressured to have.

Every woman has a story.

One of us was only fourteen years old the first time a very close friend was raped. We won't say which of us, to protect the privacy of this friend. She was alone with three men in an apartment. All of them raped her and one of them filmed it. She fled the apartment covered in bruises, wearing nothing but her jacket. She borrowed a phone from a stranger and called the police, who found her hysterically crying on the side of the road. They picked up her belongings from the apartment and took her to a Rape Crisis Centre for testing. Here, sperm from three individuals was confirmed and her bruises were photographed.

As she went to file a report, she was discouraged from opening a case. Why? Because despite evidence of intercourse, she couldn't prove that she didn't consent. She dropped the case, the three guys carried on with their lives, and she spent the next five years battling depression and anxiety while struggling to finish her education.

This friend is not alone in her experience. Nor was she our last friend or close relative to go through this type of experience.

For too many women, sexual violence and harassment feel like an unavoidable part of life. A reality so widespread that it shapes how we move through the world. In fact, it's so normal that an investigation by UN Women found that 97% of British women aged eighteen to twenty-four have been sexually harassed or assaulted.[23] Yes, you read that right. 97%.

Why did we decide to write about sexual violence in a book about money? Because money doesn't exist in a vacuum. Our ability to earn, save, invest and thrive financially is deeply connected to our safety, our autonomy and our mental health. Sexual violence disrupts all of that. It impacts a woman's ability to stay in school, to hold down a job, to build financial confidence and to trust people in positions of power. Survivors often carry the burden in silence – emotionally, physically and financially.

Ignoring this reality means ignoring one of the most invisible and unjust financial obstacles women face. It means pretending that a woman's economic life can be separated from the violence she may have experienced or is still at risk of experiencing. We can't talk honestly about closing the gender wealth gap without naming the ways that trauma derails financial stability, especially when it's trauma affecting almost all women. And we can't empower women financially without acknowledging the systems and the silence that leave survivors to carry the cost alone.

It's time to break that silence. To name what's been left unsaid. And to show that healing, safety and financial independence are deeply intertwined – and absolutely worth fighting for.

We live in a rape culture

In the UK, one in four women will experience rape or attempted rape in their lifetime.[24]

Most of these rapes are committed by someone the victim already knows, and that might be why only around 30% of rapes are reported to the police.[25] Many people still have an outdated idea of what rape looks like: a violent attack by a stranger. When there are no visible injuries, and the perpetrator is someone familiar, it's often not recognised as rape. For example, it wasn't until 1992 that marital rape was made illegal in the UK.[26]

Even though rape is now illegal, in practice it remains a crime with almost no consequence for perpetrators, and devastating consequences for survivors. In the UK, less than 1% of reported rapes lead to a conviction.[27]

Less.

Than.

1%.

These numbers speak for themselves, and they're a symptom of the rape culture we live in. It's not surprising that the previously referenced investigation by UN Women found that even though 97% of UK women aged eighteen to twenty-four have been sexually harassed, 96% did not report it.[28] Why would they? When women are not taken seriously – when we don't believe them, protect them or fight for them – we allow this violence to continue. We let it slide in classrooms, in boardrooms, in courtrooms. And over time, we stop being shocked by it. It becomes just another part of being a woman.

Ask yourself: can you name a single woman who reported a rapist and won?

Most people can't. But most of us can name men accused by multiple women who still hold power. We can name men who kept their jobs, kept their reputations, and in some cases gained even more influence. In 2024, the United States elected a man as president who had already been found liable in a civil case for sexual abuse and defamation. That's what happens when we dismiss, minimise or discredit survivors. When we reduce their pain to a 'he said, she said'. When we ask what they were wearing, what they drank, or why they didn't leave sooner. This cultural disregard sends a message, not just to victims, but to perpetrators too: *You will get away with it.*

And they do.

These numbers and facts are not local exceptions, they are symptoms of a global reality. Sexual violence is a near-universal experience for women across borders, cultures and generations. According to the CDC, more than half of all women (54.3%) in the US have experienced some form of sexual violence in their lifetime.[29] In India, government data shows that a rape is reported every fifteen minutes, and those are only the cases that make it into the official record. Worldwide, the World Health Organization estimates that around one in three women will experience physical or sexual violence in their lifetime, most often at the hands of an intimate partner. That's more than one billion women alive today.

What links these statistics isn't only the violence itself, but also the deep-rooted cultural norms that normalise it, excuse it and hide it. Whether it's a country where marital rape is still legal or a courtroom where the victim's clothing is on trial more than the perpetrator, the result is the same: silence, shame and impunity.

The risk of false accusations

We can't talk about toxic masculinity and rape culture without addressing a central claim in the manosphere: that it is men who are routinely destroyed by false rape allegations.

This is not just untrue, it's the complete opposite to reality. The people who get destroyed by rape allegations are not the perpetrators, it is the survivors. Let's get the facts straight: sexual assault is significantly under-reported.[30] Only 2–8% are estimated to be fake accusations – the same proportion of fake accusations as for other types of crime. Still, false rape accusations get a disproportionate amount of attention. Can you think of any other crime where victims are as often suspected of false allegations?

And how big *really* is the risk of being falsely accused? When looking at the number of fake rape accusations compared to the number of men, the average adult man in England and Wales has a 0.00021281% chance of being falsely accused of rape in a year.[31] Plus, even in the 0.00021281% scenario where a man gets falsely accused, there's a 99% chance he'll walk free.[32] Given that 9% of rape survivors are men, it also means that men are 230 times more likely to be raped by another man than they are to be falsely accused of rape.

One more time for the people in the back: men are 230 times more likely to be raped by another man than they are to be falsely accused of rape.

While the 0.00021281% risk of being falsely accused of rape is a big topic in the manosphere, the topic of sexual assault isn't, despite the fact that one in five American women and one in four British women will experience rape or attempted rape in their lifetime.[33,34]

The solution isn't complicated: it requires empathy, honesty and a willingness to look at the numbers with clear eyes. Yet in the manosphere, outrage over false accusations drowns out any meaningful conversation about the far more pervasive reality of sexual assault.

Regardless, it's time to shift the narrative. Instead of focusing on the 0.00021281% chance of being falsely accused of rape, let's talk about the fact that 99% of reported rapists walk free.

- 97% of UK women have been sexually harassed.[35]
- One in four UK women will experience rape or attempted rape in her lifetime.[36]
- 91% of rape survivors are women.[37]
- 99% of perpetrators are men.[38]
- 1% of reported rapes end with a felony conviction in the UK.[39]
- Men are 230 times more likely to be raped (by another man) than to be falsely accused of rape.[40]
- 33% of UK men don't think it can be considered rape if a woman has flirted on a date and then changed her mind.[41]
- 90% of rape survivors know their offender.[42]

THE COST OF TOXIC MASCULINITY

The physical and emotional harm sexual violence inflicts on survivors is devastating, and it doesn't end there. Hidden beneath the trauma is another wound that receives far less attention: the lifelong financial toll.

According to a 2025 report looking only at England and Wales, the lifetime economic cost of sexual violence committed in 2024 alone will equate to £292 billion.[43] That's seven times greater than the entire UK advertising industry that same year.[44] These figures reflect society's costs, from healthcare and criminal justice expenses to lost productivity, the need for specialist support services and the survivors' ability to work and live independently.

Zooming in, we can see how these society-wide statistics break down for individual survivors. According to the UK Office for National Statistics, 21% of survivors take time off work,[45] resulting in lost income.[46] Accessing necessary mental health support is also expensive, as long waiting times for national services push survivors towards private sessions. On top of that, legal proceedings can easily exceed £10,000 (with little guarantee of a resolution, as we have seen) plus expenses for housing, safety, travel and childcare. These expenses are overwhelmingly borne by survivors themselves, contributing to long-term economic hardship and instability. As a result, some sources estimate the lifetime cost for a victim of sexual violence to be £73,000.[47]

Across the world, we see that survivors of sexual violence are more likely to drop out of school, lose their jobs, struggle with mental and physical health and experience long-term poverty. According to research in the US, over half of survivors lose their jobs or are forced to quit in the aftermath of an assault. In South Africa, women who experienced gender-based violence were significantly less likely to be employed or financially independent, while in Australia survivors reported being four times more likely to face disruption to their education or career.

As well as psychological and physical scars, sexual violence fractures a woman's economic trajectory. It cuts into her earning potential, her independence, her safety net and her ability to build wealth over time. And when justice systems fail to hold perpetrators accountable, the burden – emotionally, practically and financially – is carried almost entirely by survivors.

This is the cost of something so common it's barely even considered remarkable. It's the price women pay, every day, for a crime that is still met with disbelief, blame and silence. That's why it needs to be talked about in a book about money. Because until the world acknowledges this reality and its consequences, women will continue to lose – emotionally, physically and financially too. Until we reckon with this, the gender wealth gap isn't just hard to close. It's designed to stay open.

Generational trauma

The poignant truth is that you don't need to have experienced sexual violence yourself for it to shape your life. For many women, the trauma lives in our families, in our cultures and in our bodies. It's passed down quietly: through stories from our loved ones, warnings that were repeated too often, or rules we internalised without questioning. *Be careful. Don't wear that. Don't walk alone. Don't trust too easily. Don't drink too much. Don't leave your drink unattended. Don't invite him in. Don't make him angry. Don't say no too loudly. Don't say yes too soon.*

At first glance, it might seem like these lessons are about safety. That they are intended to protect us. But at their core, they're about limitations – about shrinking our movements, our voices, our choices, all in response to a world that hasn't made space for us to feel safe. Over time, that limitation comes with a financial cost.

It's worth saying that generational trauma does not only belong to women. Men inherit their own burdens too. Across generations, boys have been taught that their worth lies in being strong providers, protectors and soldiers. Many were raised under the shadow of war and conscription, or pushed into breadwinner roles that left no room for vulnerability, creativity or rest. Those lessons – *don't cry, don't fail, don't fall behind* – can leave men emotionally cut off from themselves and from others. Rigid masculinity exacts its own price.

But here's the difference: while men's inherited traumas often limit their ability to connect or to seek help, women's inherited traumas have systematically limited our ability to participate fully and equally in society. One shrinks emotional possibility; the other shrinks economic and social opportunity. Both are real and both deserve acknowledgement. But only one has consistently dictated who gets to hold wealth, power and independence.

When you grow up being told that danger is everywhere and it's your job to stay safe, fear becomes the lens through which you see the world. It becomes a pattern, repeated across generations, where women are taught to value caution more than confidence. Where men are often raised to conquer the world, women are raised to survive it.

We've seen it up close. Women who chose 'safe' careers over ambitious ones, who didn't speak up at work because they were too used to being disbelieved. Women who undercharged, over-apologised, or stayed silent in negotiations because they were raised to avoid conflict at all costs. And women who never learnt to trust their financial instincts because no one ever taught them to trust themselves at all.

When you believe that the world is unsafe, and that your safety depends on staying quiet and compliant, it's very hard to imagine asking for a raise, investing your savings or starting a business. It's hard to feel like you deserve wealth, when you've inherited a story that says you're lucky just to be okay.

This is what generational trauma does: it shows up in the way we make decisions, even when we don't realise where the roots of those decisions live. It affects our sense of agency, our appetite for risk, our beliefs about what we're capable of and what we're allowed to have.

Financial empowerment doesn't start with a budget or a bank account. It starts with unlearning the limits that have been placed on us. It starts with naming the trauma that shaped the rules we were given. It starts with saying: I'm allowed to want more. I'm allowed to feel safe. I'm allowed to take up space. And I'm allowed to build a future that isn't shaped by fear.

Healing isn't just personal, it's financial. When we break the silence, we don't just honour ourselves. We change the story for the women who come next.

GO FORWARD, NEVER BACK

The struggles men face today – whether around mental health, loneliness or navigating rigid expectations of masculinity – are real, and they deserve compassion and attention. The violence that is born out of the extremity of this crisis is also, horrifyingly, real.

Yet they are not women's responsibility to fix.

It is not our job to shrink back, to give in, to absorb the cost of supporting men at the expense of our own progress. For too long, women have been expected to play small, smooth the way and do invisible labour so men could succeed. We didn't come this far to step aside the moment men struggle to manage life without our unpaid and often unseen support. Feminism is not about bringing men down; it's about creating an equal society where both men and women can thrive. Challenging inequality and toxic masculinity benefits everyone – including men, because freedom from rigid roles is likely as liberating for them as it is for us. The most helpful thing we can do for the men we love is to hold them to higher standards, challenge them to rise to the occasion – and believe they can. This isn't punishment; it's accountability.

We must focus on building financial independence, because money equals power, and power equals freedom. In a time where women's rights are under attack around the world and where toxic masculinity is growing like wildfire, women must prioritise financial security and use money strategically to protect their autonomy. True independence means not being constrained, controlled or forced to compromise your life or ambitions. This isn't just about personal gain: financial leverage is the foundation for choice, opportunity and equality. By taking control of our money, we safeguard ourselves, our future and future generations, ensuring that progress can't be reversed. That's exactly why we built Female Invest: to give women the tools, knowledge and confidence to take ownership of their financial future. We've seen it over and over again: nothing is more transformative, empowering or powerful than when women take control of their money – and with it, their lives. And when women are financially secure, entire families and communities benefit too.

So where do we go from here? The answer is simple: forward, never back. This is not the time to lower our standards, soften our voices, or shrink ourselves out of sympathy for men struggling to adapt to a world that no longer guarantees them automatic privilege. For centuries, women have been expected to play small, to please, to serve. We didn't fight this hard, break down this many barriers and reclaim this much ground just to give it all up the moment men are challenged to stand on their own.

Because here's the truth: this is not women's responsibility to carry. It is work men must lead. Toxic masculinity traps men too, robbing them of vulnerability, intimacy and the chance to live fuller lives. The way we support the men we love – our fathers, brothers, partners and sons – is not to fear their fragility but to hold them to higher standards. To believe they are capable of rising to the occasion, and to demand that they do.

That's how progress is made. That's how a more equitable, safe and thriving future is built: not by women stepping down, but with men stepping up.

That's why money matters. That's why this book matters, and this chapter in particular. Financial independence is what allows women to prioritise themselves, to protect their autonomy, and to never be forced into compromise. If we step back now – if we start lowering the bar out of sympathy for men's struggles – we risk undoing everything we've fought for.

This moment demands strength, clarity and courage. It's not about putting men down, it's about challenging them to rise higher. Because when they do, everyone wins.

CONCLUSION: WHAT WILL YOU DO NEXT?

By Anna-Sophie, Camilla and Emma

By now, we hope that you've learnt a lot and that these pages have sparked new ways of thinking about money, power and the invisible forces that shape our financial lives. You've seen how history has written women out of the story, how stereotypes still whisper in the background of our choices, and how systems quietly reinforce inequality. Understanding these dynamics is powerful, but it's only the beginning. Real change doesn't happen in theory. Real change requires action.

That action starts with you. It involves speaking up in conversations where silence has long been the norm. It involves challenging stereotypes, whether it's an offhand comment at work, outdated assumptions at the dinner table or even the quiet voice of doubt inside yourself. It involves taking concrete steps in your own life: setting financial goals, building independence and refusing to shrink back from the opportunities that money can unlock.

It won't be easy. The barriers you'll encounter are real, and sometimes they show up in ways that seem invisible until you name them. You may be met with resistance: the raised eyebrows, the dismissive remarks, the systems designed to make progress slower than it should be. But every step matters. Every conversation you start, every stereotype you refuse to accept and every choice you make to stand in your financial power creates ripples that extend far beyond you.

In all honesty, we've thought a lot about the potential repercussions of writing this book. About the criticism, the labels, the consequences. Speaking up has always carried risk for women, because whenever women step forward to claim their place, the world has pushed back.

History has taught women what happens when we dare to speak up. Women who raise their voices have been silenced, shamed, or punished for centuries. From the witches burned at the stake for their 'dangerous' ideas, to the suffragettes mocked and imprisoned for demanding the vote, to modern-day women 'cancelled' for stepping out of line, our culture has a long track record of disciplining outspoken women.

The truth is, women are routinely held to higher standards. A man can be controversial and he will likely be branded 'bold'. A woman can say the exact same thing and be branded 'difficult'.

A man can make a mistake and recover. A woman can make the same mistake and never live it down. Cancellation isn't new, it's just wearing new clothes.

Even the very language we use has been shaped to keep women in their place. Take the word *gossip*. Today, it's often used to trivialise women's conversations, as if what women say to each other is silly or meaningless. But historically, the word had an entirely different meaning. *Gossip* comes from the Old English *god-sib*, meaning 'godparent': a close, trusted friend, often a woman present at a birth. Over time, as women gathered in kitchens, at wells, or during childbirth, their conversations became threatening to a male-dominated society. Their bonds were mocked and diminished by turning the word 'gossip' into something frivolous and shameful. It was a linguistic weapon, a way to devalue women's voices and discourage them from coming together.

That pattern has never really gone away. The ridicule, the double standards, the attempts to shrink women's voices. All of it persists, just in updated forms.

And yet, we chose to write this book anyway. Because silence has never protected women, and because the cost of staying quiet is far higher than the risk of speaking up. Yes, there was fear in writing these pages. But there is also conviction. Conviction that change only happens when women keep talking, keep questioning, and keep raising the standards for ourselves and for the world around us.

This book is an invitation. We hope it has challenged the way you think about the central pieces of a woman's life: money, power, health, relationships, freedom. We hope it continues to spark conversations you've never had before, or makes you see familiar ones in a new light.

Change is possible. Starting today, every choice you make,

every habit you build, every rule you challenge brings you closer to the life of independence and freedom you deserve. With every woman who challenges the narrative and steps into her financial power, we get one step closer to financial equality.

But change has never come from waiting. It comes from persistence, from ordinary people refusing to accept the status quo and choosing, again and again, to act. That's the invitation we want to leave you with: not only to think differently, but to live differently. To take what you've learnt and carry it into the world, where it can transform your own life and the lives of the women who come after you.

That's why this book exists.

Now, we pass the torch to you. What will you do next?

ACKNOWLEDGEMENTS

No book is ever a solitary effort. Every word, every idea and every page is shaped by the incredible people who work alongside us, offering guidance, support and inspiration. This book is no exception, and we are deeply grateful to everyone who helped us on our journey to publication.

To Anna Argenio and Naomi Morris Omori, our incredible UK editors, thank you for helping bring the idea behind this book to life. Your insight, thoughtful feedback and unwavering support made the process not only possible but joyful. A heartfelt thanks also to Javerya Iqbal and the rest of the amazing team at Orion Books for helping this book reach the world.

A special thank you to Julie Bloch Korsemann, our Danish editor, who has been with us through both the challenging and exciting moments. Your belief in us, sound advice, flexibility and positivity have meant so much. And to Mette Lund, Mette Andersen and the rest of the team at Lindhardt og Ringhof: thank you for your dedication to getting our books into the hands of women across the country.

To Oscar Janson-Smith, our extraordinary agent, thank you for finding the perfect home for this book. It's rare to find someone as dedicated, capable and hardworking as you. You have been a trusted partner at every step of the journey, and we are endlessly grateful.

To our community, thank you for inspiring us and cheering us on when the journey felt daunting. Your support made sure we never felt alone. Much of what is in this book comes from you. Your questions, your curiosity and your high standards have pushed us to aim higher.

To our partners, thank you for encouraging us to dream bigger, for challenging traditional gender roles, and for believing in us even when it meant sacrificing time together. It's not always easy to be with someone who tries to turn the world on its head and appreciate having you as co-captains on this journey.

Finally, thank you to our parents, for raising us to believe that we could be anything, and for instilling the confidence and courage that allowed us to write this book in the first place.

ABOUT THE AUTHORS

Camilla Falkenberg, **Emma Due Bitz** and **Anna-Sophie Hartvigsen** are the founders of Female Invest, a global financial educator targeting women. Through their subscription business, which has members in more than 130 countries, they educate women on personal finance and investing with a mission to close the financial gender gap. More than 100,000 women have taken their courses, and they are listed on the *Forbes* 30 Under 30 List within finance, having raised over $23 million in a world where women (sadly) raise less than 2% of funding. They are the winners of the Cartier Women's Initiative, the world's largest startup competition, and authored the international bestseller *Girls Just Wanna Have Funds*. Their work has been featured in *Forbes*, *Vogue*, *Harper's Bazaar*, *Financial Times* and many others.

NOTES

Introduction

1 World Economic Forum. (2026). *The Global Gender Parity Sprint to 2030: How we are scaling parity and opportunity for 1.5 million women.* Retrieved from https://www.weforum.org/impact/global-gender-parity-sprint-to-2030-scaling-parity-and-opportunity-for-women/ [last accessed: 06 Feb 2025]

2 Abode Financial. (2025). *The gender pension gap.* Retrieved from https://abodefinancial.co.uk/blog/gender-pension-gap/ [last accessed: 06 Oct 2025]

3 The Co-operative Bank. (2024). *The pink tax: Why women are paying more for their essentials.* Retrieved from https://www.co-operativebank.co.uk/content-hub/articles-and-advice/pink-tax-women-paying-more-for-their-essentials/ [last accessed: 06 Oct 2025]

4 Oxfam International. (n.d.). *Not all gaps are created equal: The true value of care work.* Retrieved from https://www.oxfam.org/en/not-all-gaps-are-created-equal-true-value-care-work [last accessed: 06 Oct 2025]

Married Men Are the Real Gold-diggers

1 British Sociological Association. (2017). *Women do more housework than men – even when their partners are unemployed.* Retrieved from https://www.britsoc.co.uk/media-centre/press-releases/2017/march/women-do-more-housework-than-men-even-when-their-partners-are-unemployed/ [last accessed: 06 Oct 2025]

2 Bare Marriage. (2023). *Are 70% of divorces really caused by women divorcing frivolously?* Retrieved from https://baremarriage.com/2023/11/are-70-of-divorces-really-caused-by-women-divorcing-frivolously/ [last accessed: 06 Oct 2025]

3 Carroll, L. (2018). *Men more likely to leave spouse who has cancer, study shows. NBC News.* Retrieved from https://www.nbcnews.com/health/health-news/men-more-likely-leave-spouse-who-has-cancer-flna1c9450218 [last accessed: 06 Oct 2025]

4 Khazan, O. (2019). *Women happier without children or a spouse, says happiness expert. The Guardian.* Retrieved from https://www.theguardian.com/lifeandstyle/2019/may/25/women-happier-without-children-or-a-spouse-happiness-expert [last accessed: 06 Oct 2025]

5 Global Fund for Women. (n.d.). *A brief history of marriage and money.* Retrieved from https://exhibitions.globalfundforwomen.org/economica/marriage-and-money/brief-history-marriage [last accessed: 06 Oct 2025]

6 The Verdict Online. (2024). *The Napoleonic Code: France's quiet revolution.* Retrieved from https://www.theverdictonline.org/post/the-napoleonic-code-france-s-quiet-revolution [last accessed: 06 Oct 2025]

7 Euronews. (2019). *Germany celebrates 100 years of women's suffrage.* Retrieved from https://www.euronews.com/2019/01/17/germany-celebrates-100-years-of-women-s-suffrage [last accessed: 06 Oct 2025]

8 Mannion, M. (2025). *Women in wealth throughout history: A United States timeline.* Retrieved from https://www.chase.com/personal/investments/learning-and-insights/article/women-in-wealth-throughout-history-a-united-states-timeline [last accessed: 06 Oct 2025]

9 United Nations Population Fund (UNFPA). (2021). *State of World Population 2021.* Retrieved from https://www.unfpa.org/sowp-2021 [last accessed: 06 Oct 2025]

10 Ratcliffe, R. (2021). *'Marry your rapist' laws in 20 countries still allow perpetrators to escape justice. Guardian.* Retrieved from https://www.theguardian.com/global-development/2021/apr/14/marry-your-rapist-laws-in-20-countries-still-allow-perpetrators-to-escape-justice [last accessed: 06 Oct 2025]

11 UK Parliament. (n.d.). *Marriage: property and children.* Retrieved from https://www.parliament.uk/about/living-heritage/transformingsociety/private-lives/relationships/overview/propertychildren/ [last accessed 08 Oct 2025]

12 Hochschild, A., & Machung, A. (2012). *The second shift: Working families and the revolution at home.* Retrieved from https://discovered.ed.ac.uk/discovery/fulldisplay/alma9925295396302466/44UOE_INST:44UOE_VU2 [last accessed: 06 Oct 2025]

13 Wezerek, G., & Ghodsee, K. R. (2020). *Women's unpaid labor is worth $10,900,000,000,000. The New York Times.* Retrieved from https://www.nytimes.com/interactive/2020/03/04/opinion/women-unpaid-labor.html [last accessed: 06 Oct 2025]

14 Cherie Blair Foundation. (n.d.). *Unpaid care work.* Retrieved from https://

cherieblairfoundation.org/news-list/unpaid-care-work/ [last accessed: 06 Oct 2025]

15 Pew Research Center. (2023). *In a Growing Share of U.S. Marriages, Husbands and Wives Earn About the Same.* Retrieved from https://www.pewresearch.org/social-trends/2023/04/13/in-a-growing-share-of-u-s-marriages-husbands-and-wives-earn-about-the-same/ [last accessed: 09 Jan 2026]

16 UBS. (2018). *UBS reveals top reason married women step aside in long-term financial decisions: They believe their husbands know more [Press release].* Retrieved from https://www.ubs.com/global/en/media/display-page-ndp/en-20180514-ubs-reveals-top-reason.html [last accessed: 06 Oct 2025]

17 UBS. (2018). *UBS reveals top reason married women step aside in long-term financial decisions: They believe their husbands know more [Press release].* Retrieved from https://www.ubs.com/global/en/media/display-page-ndp/en-20180514-ubs-reveals-top-reason.html [last accessed: 06 Oct 2025]

18 Global Fund for Women. (n.d.). *A brief history of marriage and money.* Retrieved from https://exhibitions.globalfundforwomen.org/economica/marriage-and-money/brief-history-marriage [last accessed: 06 Oct 2025]

19 NPR. (2014). *Same-sex couples may have more egalitarian relationships.* Retrieved from https://www.npr.org/2014/12/29/373835114/same-sex-couples-may-have-more-egalitarian-relationships [last accessed: 06 Oct 2025]

20 World Economic Forum. (2017). *Gender pay gap: The 'lesbian premium'.* Retrieved from https://www.weforum.org/stories/2017/03/gender-pay-gap-lesbian-premium/ [last accessed: 06 Oct 2025]

21 Bauer, G. (2018). *Gender roles, comparative advantages, and the life course. Frontiers in Sociology, 3,* 1–12. https://doi.org/10.3389/fsoc.2018.00017 Retrieved from https://pmc.ncbi.nlm.nih.gov/articles/PMC6223479/ [last accessed: 06 Oct 2025]

22 The Jimenez Law Firm. (2022). *Why women initiate divorce more often than men.* Retrieved from https://www.thejimenezlawfirm.com/why-women-initiate-divorce-more-often-than-men/ [last accessed: 06 Oct 2025]

23 Pensions Age. (2020). *Divorced women's retirement savings 75% smaller than male counterparts.* Retrieved from https://www.pensionsage.com/pa/Divorced-womens-retirement-savings-75-smaller-than-male-counterparts.php [last accessed: 06 Oct 2025]

24 Creative Planning. (2022). *How women are financially affected by divorce.* Retrieved from https://www.creativeplanning.com/insights/financial-planning/how-women-are-financially-affected-by-divorce/ [last accessed: 06 Oct 2025]

25 Russell, J., & White, J. (2023). *The reality behind widowhood: The time to start preparing for it is now. Baird Trust.* Retrieved from https://www.bairdtrust.com/news-insights/2023/07/the-reality-behind-widowhood/ [last accessed: 06 Oct 2025]

26 Hahn, E. A., Cichy, K. E., Almeida, D. M., & Haley, W. E. (2011). *Time use and well-being in older widows: Adaptation and resilience. Journal of Women & Aging, 23*(2), 149–159. https://doi.org/10.1080/08952841.2011.561139 Retrieved from https://pmc.ncbi.nlm.nih.gov/articles/PMC3485066/ [last accessed: 06 Oct 2025]

27 Glantz, M. J., Chamberlain, M. C., Liu, Q., Hsieh, C.-C., Edwards, K. R., Van Horn, A., & Recht, L. (2009). *Gender disparity in the rate of partner abandonment in patients with serious medical illness. Cancer, 115*(22), 5237–5242. https://doi.org/10.1002/cncr.24577 Retrieved from https://pubmed.ncbi.nlm.nih.gov/19645027/ [last accessed: 06 Oct 2025]

28 DePaulo, B. (2025). *Why more marriages end when wives get sick than when husbands do. Psychology Today.* Retrieved from https://www.psychologytoday.com/gb/blog/living-single/202503/more-marriages-end-when-wives-get-sick-than-when-husbands-do [last accessed: 06 Oct 2025]

Health is Wealth

1 World Economic Forum. (2024). *Closing the Women's Health Gap: A $1 Trillion Opportunity to Improve Lives and Economies.* Geneva: World Economic Forum. Retrieved from https://www3.weforum.org/docs/WEF_Closing_the_Women%E2%80%99s_Health_Gap_2024.pdf [last accessed: 06 Oct 2025]

2 Pisetsky, D. S. (2019,). *Women diagnosed years later than men for same diseases. The Rheumatologist.* Retrieved from https://www.the-rheumatologist.org/article/women-diagnosed-years-later-than-men-for-same-diseases/ [last accessed: 06 Oct 2025]

3 UK Centre for Process Innovation (CPI). (2025). *The gender gap persists in health research: Here's what we can do to close it.* Retrieved from https://www.uk-cpi.com/blog/the-gender-gap-persists-in-health-research-heres-what-we-can-do-to-close-it [last accessed: 06 Oct 2025]

4 360info. (2024). *Made by men, for men: Why medicine's gender bias matters.* Retrieved from https://360info.org/made-by-men-for-men-why-medicines-gender-bias-matters/ [last accessed: 06 Oct 2025]

5 Integrated Care Journal. (2024). *Women spending 1.5 times more: Personal health report finds.* Retrieved from https://integratedcarejournal.com/women-spending-1-5-times-more-personal-health-report-finds/ [last accessed: 06 Oct 2025]

6 NHS Confederation. (2024). *Economic case for investing in women's health services revealed.* Retrieved from https://www.nhsconfed.org/news/economic-case-investing-womens-health-services-revealed [last accessed: 06 Oct 2025]

7 UK Centre for Process Innovation (CPI). (2025). *The gender gap persists in health research: Here's what we can do to close it.* Retrieved from https://www.uk-cpi.com/blog/the-gender-gap-persists-in-health-research-heres-what-we-can-do-to-close-it [last accessed: 06 Oct 2025]

8 McKinsey Health Institute. (2024). *New report highlights $1 trillion potential of closing women's health gap.* Retrieved from https://www.mckinsey.com/mhi/media-center/new-report-highlights-one-trillion-potential-of-closing-womens-health-gap [last accessed: 06 Oct 2025]

9 Yale Medicine. (n.d.). *Uveitis.* Retrieved from https://www.yalemedicine.org/conditions/uveitis [last accessed: 06 Oct 2025]

10 European Institute for Gender Equality (EIGE). (2019). *Gender Equality Index 2019 Report: Women live longer, in poorer health.* Retrieved from https://eige.europa.eu/publications-resources/toolkits-guides/gender-equality-index-2019-report/women-live-longer-poorer-health [last accessed: 06 Oct 2025]

11 World Economic Forum. (2024). *Women's health at Davos 2024.* Retrieved from https://www.weforum.org/stories/2024/01/women-health-davos-2024/ [last accessed: 06 Oct 2025]

12 Batulan, Z., Bhimla, A., & Higginbotham, E. J. (Eds.). (2024). *Advancing research on chronic conditions in women.* In National Academies of Sciences, Engineering, and Medicine. *Advancing research on chronic conditions in women.* Washington, DC: National Academies Press. https://www.ncbi.nlm.nih.gov/books/NBK607719/ [last accessed: 06 Oct 2025]

13 National Academies of Sciences, Engineering, and Medicine. (2024). *Significant lack of data and research on chronic conditions affecting women is hindering diagnosis, treatment, and prevention.* Retrieved from https://www.nationalacademies.org/news/2024/07/significant-lack-of-data-and-research-on-chronic-conditions-affecting-women-is-hindering-diagnosis-treatment-and-prevention-report-calls-for-enhanced-nih-research-effort [last accessed: 06 Oct 2025]

14 Boulder Community Health. (2025). *Endometriosis: The chronic condition that's more than pain.* Retrieved from https://www.bch.org/latest-news/2025/march/endometriosis-the-chronic-condition-that-s-more-/ [last accessed: 06 Oct 2025]

15 Albert, P. R. (2015). *Why is depression more prevalent in women? Journal of psychiatry & neuroscience: JPN, 40*(4), 219–221. https://doi.org/10.1503/jpn.150205 Retrieved from https://pmc.ncbi.nlm.nih.gov/articles/PMC4478054/ [last accessed: 06 Oct 2025]

16 Mayo Clinic. (n.d.). *Depression: Symptoms and causes.* Retrieved from https://www.mayoclinic.org/diseases-conditions/depression/in-depth/depression/art-20047725 [last accessed: 06 Oct 2025]

17 Coleman, T. (2024). *Women's pain is ignored in health care. The Week (US).* Retrieved from https://theweek.com/health/women-pain-ignored-health-care [last accessed: 06 Oct 2025]

18 This is from the data that women wait 48.1 minutes on average vs men who wait 37.2 minutes on average, thus the calculated the difference is 29%. Source: Banco, D., Chang, J., Talmor, N., Wadhera, P., Mukhopadhyay, A., Lu, X., Dong, S., Lu, Y., Betensky, R. A., Blecker, S., Safdar, B., & Reynolds, H. R. (2022). *Sex and race differences in the evaluation and treatment of young adults presenting to the emergency department with chest pain. Journal of the American Heart Association, 11*(10), e024199. https://doi.org/10.1161/JAHA.121.024199 [last accessed: 06 Oct 2025]

19 Maserejian, N. N., Link, C. L., Lutfey, K. L., Marceau, L. D., & McKinlay, J. B. (2009). *Disparities in physicians' interpretations of heart disease symptoms by patient gender: Results of a video vignette factorial experiment. Journal of Women's Health, 18*(10), 1661–1667. https://doi.org/10.1089/jwh.2008.1007 Retrieved from https://pmc.ncbi.nlm.nih.gov/articles/PMC2825679/ [last accessed: 06 Oct 2025]

20 BBC Future. (2018). *The inequality in how women are treated for pain.* Retrieved from https://www.bbc.com/future/article/20180518-the-inequality-in-how-women-are-treated-for-pain [last accessed: 06 Oct 2025]

21 Novo Nordisk Foundation Center for Protein Research (CPR). (2019). *Study across diseases: Women are diagnosed later than men.* University of Copenhagen. Retrieved from https://www.cpr.ku.dk/cpr-news/2019/study-across-diseases-women-are-diagnosed-later-than-men/ [last accessed: 06 Oct 2025]

22 House of Lords Library. (2023). *Maternal mortality rates in the Black*

community (UK). Retrieved from https://lordslibrary.parliament.uk/maternal-mortality-rates-in-the-black-community/ [last accessed: 06 Oct 2025]

23 Yang, Y., Reid, M. C., Grol-Prokopczyk, H., & Pillemer, K. (2021). *Racial-ethnic disparities in pain intensity and interference among middle-aged and older U.S. adults. The Journals of Gerontology: Series A, Biological Sciences and Medical Sciences,* 77(2), e74–e81. https://doi.org/10.1093/gerona/glab207 Retrieved from https://pmc.ncbi.nlm.nih.gov/articles/PMC8824568/ [last accessed: 06 Oct 2025]

24 Salam, M. (2018). *For Serena Williams, Childbirth Was a Harrowing Ordeal. She's Not Alone.* https://www.nytimes.com/2018/01/11/sports/tennis/serena-williams-baby-vogue.html [last accessed: 12 Dec 2025]

25 Swetlitz, I. (2016). *Some medical students still think Black patients feel less pain than Whites. STAT News.* Retrieved from https://www.statnews.com/2016/04/04/medical-students-beliefs-race-pain/ [last accessed: 06 Oct 2025]

26 Hoffman, K. M., et al. (2016). *Racial bias in pain assessment and treatment recommendations and false beliefs about biological differences between Blacks and Whites. Proceedings of the National Academy of Sciences, 113*(16), 4296–4301. Retrieved from https://pubmed.ncbi.nlm.nih.gov/27044069/ [last accessed: 06 Oct 2025]

27 Stromberg, J. (2015). *'Bicycle face': A 19th-century health problem made up to scare women away from biking. Vox.* Retrieved from https://www.vox.com/2015/3/24/8277831/bicycle-face [last accessed: 06 Oct 2025]

28 McGill University Office for Science and Society. (2020). *Moral and medical panic over bicycles.* Retrieved from https://www.mcgill.ca/oss/article/history-did-you-know/moral-and-medical-panic-over-bicycles [last accessed: 06 Oct 2025]

29 *History Detective Podcast.* (2021). *Bicycle face.* Retrieved from https://historydetectivepodcast.com/bicycle-face/ [last accessed: 06 Oct 2025]

30 Office of Research on Women's Health (NIH). (n.d.). *History of women's inclusion in clinical research.* Retrieved from https://orwh.od.nih.gov/toolkit/recruitment/history [last accessed: 06 Oct 2025]

31 Courchesne, M., Manrique, G., Bernier, L., Moussa, L., Cresson, J., Gutzeit, A., Froehlich, J. M., Koh, D.-M., Chartrand-Lefebvre, C., & Matoori, S. (2023). *Gender differences in pharmacokinetics: A perspective on contrast agents. ACS Pharmacology & Translational Science,* 7(1), 8–17. https://doi.org/10.1021/acsptsci.3c00116 Retrieved from https://pmc.ncbi.nlm.nih.gov/articles/PMC10789139/ [last accessed: 06 Oct 2025]

32 Soldin, O. P., & Mattison, D. R. (2009). *Sex differences in pharmacokinetics and pharmacodynamics. Clinical pharmacokinetics, 48*(3), 143–157. https://doi.org/10.2165/00003088-200948030-00001 Retrieved from https://pmc.ncbi.nlm.nih.gov/articles/PMC3644551/ [last accessed: 06 Oct 2025]

33 Harvard Health Publishing. (2017). *Women and pain: Disparities in experience and treatment. Harvard Medical School.* Retrieved from https://www.health.harvard.edu/blog/women-and-pain-disparities-in-experience-and-treatment-2017100912562 [last accessed: 06 Oct 2025]

34 UK Centre for Process Innovation (CPI). (2025). *The gender gap persists in health research: Here's what we can do to close it.* Retrieved from https://www.uk-cpi.com/blog/the-gender-gap-persists-in-health-research-heres-what-we-can-do-to-close-it [last accessed: 06 Oct 2025]

35 Cawthera, E. (2023). *Q&A: How can medical science better serve women? Imperial College London.* Retrieved from https://www.imperial.ac.uk/news/247194/qa-how-medical-science-better-serve/ [last accessed: 06 Oct 2025]

36 Slawson, (2019). *Women have been woefully neglected: Does medical science have a gender problem? Guardian.* Retrieved from https://www.theguardian.com/education/2019/dec/18/women-have-been-woefully-neglected-does-medical-science-have-a-gender-problem [last accessed: 06 Oct 2025]

37 The Brainy Insights. (2024). *Erectile dysfunction drugs market report.* Retrieved from https://www.thebrainyinsights.com/report/erectile-dysfunction-drugs-market-13700 [last accessed: 06 Oct 2025]

38 GlobalData Healthcare. (2024). *Endometriosis market forecast 2034. Clinical Trials Arena.* Retrieved from https://www.clinicaltrialsarena.com/analyst-comment/endometriosis-market-forecast-7mm-2034/ [last accessed: 06 Oct 2025]

39 Bailey, P. (1966). *Hysteria: The history of a disease. Archives of General Psychiatry, 14*(3), 332–333. https://doi.org/10.1001/archpsyc.1966.01730090108024 Retrieved from https://jamanetwork.com/journals/jamapsychiatry/article-abstract/488986 [last accessed: 06 Oct 2025]

40 Tasca, C., Rapetti, M., Carta, M. G., & Fadda, B. (2012). *Women and hysteria in the history of mental health. Clinical practice and epidemiology in mental health: CP & EMH, 8*, 110–119. https://doi.org/10.2174/1745017901208010110 Retrieved from https://pmc.ncbi.nlm.nih.gov/articles/PMC3480686/ [last accessed: 06 Oct 2025]

41 Medical News Today. (2020). *The controversy of female hysteria.* Retrieved

from https://www.medicalnewstoday.com/articles/the-controversy-of-female-hysteria [last accessed: 06 Oct 2025]

42 A lobotomy is a type of brain surgery that involves severing connections in the brain's prefrontal cortex, often with the aim of altering a person's behaviour or emotional state. It was once used to treat mental illnesses but frequently resulted in severe personality changes and cognitive impairments.

43 Patients were subjected to high-voltage electric currents, causing seizures and often leading to memory loss and cognitive decline.

44 Horwitz, R. (2020). *Medical vibrators and the treatment of female hysteria. The Embryo Project Encyclopedia (Arizona State University).* Retrieved from https://embryo.asu.edu/pages/medical-vibrators-treatment-female-hysteria [last accessed: 06 Oct 2025]

45 Backman, I. (2024). *From hysteria to empowerment: Women's health through the ages. Yale Medicine Magazine.* Retrieved from https://medicine.yale.edu/news/yale-medicine-magazine/article/from-hysteria-to-empowerment/ [last accessed: 06 Oct 2025]

46 Hope, G. (2024). *A troubled past: The problematic history of mental healthcare for women.* Retrieved from https://www.galenhope.com/uncategorized/a-troubled-past-the-problematic-history-of-mental-healthcare-for-women/ [last accessed: 06 Oct 2025]

47 Horwitz, R. (2020). *Medical vibrators and the treatment of female hysteria. The Embryo Project Encyclopedia (Arizona State University).* Retrieved from https://embryo.asu.edu/pages/medical-vibrators-treatment-female-hysteria [last accessed: 06 Oct 2025]

48 Evon, D. (2016). *Reasons for admission to insane asylums in the 19th century. Snopes.* Retrieved from https://www.snopes.com/fact-check/reasons-admission-insane-asylum-1800s/ [last accessed: 06 Oct 2025]

49 The same brain surgery as described before.

50 Tone, A., & Koziol, M. (2018). *(F)ailing women in psychiatry: Lessons from a painful past. Canadian Medical Association Journal (CMAJ), 190*(20), E624–E625. https://doi.org/10.1503/cmaj.171277 Retrieved from https://pmc.ncbi.nlm.nih.gov/articles/PMC5962395/ [last accessed: 06 Oct 2025]

51 Atkins, H. (2022). *Mother's little helper: The history of Valium.* Retrieved from https://www.historyhit.com/mothers-little-helper-the-history-of-valium/ [last accessed: 06 Oct 2025]

52 Bodea, M., & Davies, M. (2025). *Silence, sexism and stigma: The state of*

working-age women's health in England. Nuffield Trust – QualityWatch. Retrieved from https://www.nuffieldtrust.org.uk/news-item/silence-sexism-and-stigma-the-state-of-working-age-women-s-health-in-england [last accessed: 06 Oct 2025]

53 UK Government. (2022). *Results of the Women's Health: Let's Talk About It survey. Department of Health and Social Care.* Retrieved from https://www.gov.uk/government/calls-for-evidence/womens-health-strategy-call-for-evidence/outcome/results-of-the-womens-health-lets-talk-about-it-survey [last accessed: 06 Oct 2025]

54 UK Government. (2022). *Results of the Women's Health: Let's Talk About It survey. Department of Health and Social Care.* Retrieved from https://www.gov.uk/government/calls-for-evidence/womens-health-strategy-call-for-evidence/outcome/results-of-the-womens-health-lets-talk-about-it-survey [last accessed: 06 Oct 2025]

55 Chowdhry, A. (2023). *Midi Health: Women's midlife healthcare company closes $25 million. Pulse 2.0.* Retrieved from https://pulse2.com/midi-health-womens-midlife-healthcare-company-closes-25-million/ [last accessed: 06 Oct 2025]

56 Catalyst. (2024). *Women call for more menopause support in the workplace in new global survey. Catalyst.* Retrieved from https://www.catalyst.org/about/newsroom/2024/menopause-workplace-support-global [last accessed: 06 Oct 2025]

57 UK Government. (2024). *Civil service sickness absence: 2023 report. Cabinet Office.* Retrieved from https://www.gov.uk/government/publications/civil-service-sickness-absence-2023/civil-service-sickness-absence-2023-report [last accessed: 06 Oct 2025]

58 HRD Connect. (2024). *UK loses 150 million working days due to lack of workplace support for women's health. HRD Connect.* Retrieved from https://www.hrdconnect.com/2024/02/22/uk-loses-150-million-working-days-due-to-lack-of-workplace-support-for-womens-health/ [last accessed: 06 Oct 2025]

59 Endometriosis UK. (2024). *Endometriosis UK responds to new NHS Confederation report on women's health economics: Investing 51%. Endometriosis UK.* Retrieved from https://www.endometriosis-uk.org/endometriosis-uk-respond-new-nhs-confederation-report-womens-health-economics-investing-51-cent [last accessed: 06 Oct 2025]

60 Furst, J. (2023). *Mayo Clinic study puts price tag on cost of menopause symptoms for women in the workplace. Mayo Clinic News Network.* Retrieved from https://newsnetwork.mayoclinic.org/discussion/

mayo-clinic-study-puts-price-tag-on-cost-of-menopause-symptoms-for-women-in-the-workplace/ [last accessed: 06 Oct 2025]
61 McKinsey Health Institute. (2024). *New report highlights $1 trillion potential of closing the women's health gap. McKinsey & Company.* Retrieved from https://www.mckinsey.com/mhi/media-center/new-report-highlights-one-trillion-potential-of-closing-womens-health-gap [last accessed: 06 Oct 2025]
62 Gaffney, T. (2023). *Women spend 20% more per year on out-of-pocket health costs, says report. STAT News.* Retrieved from https://www.statnews.com/2023/09/29/female-patients-medical-expenses/ [last accessed: 06 Oct 2025]
63 Gordon, D. (2023). *Women pay $15 billion more than men for medical costs, new report shows. Forbes.* Retrieved from https://www.forbes.com/sites/debgordon/2023/09/26/women-pay-15-billion-more-than-men-for-medical-costs-new-report-shows/ [last accessed: 06 Oct 2025]
64 Williams, Z. (2024). *760,000 women in UK waiting for gynaecological appointment? That's just the tip of the iceberg. Guardian.* Retrieved from https://www.theguardian.com/commentisfree/2024/nov/19/760000-women-uk-waiting-gynaecological-appointment-tip-iceberg [last accessed: 06 Oct 2025]
65 Blaazer, G. (2024). *Women spending 1.5 times more than men on personal health, report finds. Integrated Care Journal.* Retrieved from https://integrated-carejournal.com/women-spending-1-5-times-more-personal-health-report-finds/ [last accessed: 06 Oct 2025]
66 Rubin, S. (2025). *Gender gap in health benefits: Women more likely to prioritise private healthcare. YuLife.* Retrieved from https://yulife.com/blog/gender-gap-health-benefits/ [last accessed: 06 Oct 2025]
67 https://www.pharmacytimes.com/view/fun-fact-unfortunately-chain-saws-were-invented-for-childbirth
Felton, J. (2021). *We Regret To Inform You That Chainsaws Were Originally Invented For Childbirth. IFLScience.* https://www.iflscience.com/health-and-medicine/we-regret-to-inform-you-that-chainsaws-were-originally-invented-for-childbirth/
The chain saw – a Scottish invention. Scottish Medical Journal. 2004; 49(2): 72–5. doi: 10.1177/003693300404900218

Money and Motherhood

1 Vagni, G., & Breen, R. (2021). *Earnings and income penalties for motherhood: Estimates for British women using the individual synthetic control method. European Sociological Review, 37*(5), 834–848. https://doi.org/10.1093/esr/jcab014 Retrieved from https://academic.oup.com/esr/article/37/5/834/6325498 [last accessed: 08 Oct 2025]

2 McFall, M. R. (2024). *What is the motherhood penalty? New gender pay gap report explained. Newsweek.* Retrieved from https://www.newsweek.com/motherhood-penalty-report-gender-pay-gap-debate-fatherhood-bonus-1919965 [last accessed 08 Oct 2025]

3 WeAreTheCity. (2023). *Careers after babies report highlights alarming statistics for women returning to work after having children. WeAreTheCity.* Retrieved from https://wearethecity.com/careers-after-babies-report-highlights-alarming-statistics-for-women-returning-to-work-after-having-children/ [last accessed 08 Oct 2025]

4 Royal London. (2024). *The pensions parenthood penalty holding women back. Royal London Press Release.* Retrieved from https://www.royallondon.com/about-us/media/media-centre/press-releases/press-releases-2024/january/the-pensions-parenthood-penalty-holding-women-back/ [last accessed 08 Oct 2025]

5 Labour Research Department. (2025). *Discrimination worsens for pregnant employees. Labour Research Department.* Retrieved from https://www.lrd.org.uk/free-read/discrimination-worsens-pregnant-employees [last accessed 08 Oct 2025]

6 Labour Research Department. (2025). *Discrimination worsens for pregnant employees. Labour Research Department.* Retrieved from https://www.lrd.org.uk/free-read/discrimination-worsens-pregnant-employees [last accessed 08 Oct 2025]

7 Brown, L. (2018, September 27). *A fifth of HR professionals admit motherhood affects promotion prospects. People Management.* Retrieved from https://www.peoplemanagement.co.uk/article/1746791/fifth-hr-professionals-admit-motherhood-affects-promotion-prospects [last accessed 08 Oct 2025]

8 Torres, A. J. C., Barbosa-Silva, L., Oliveira-Silva, L. C., Miziara, O. P. P., Guahy, U. C. R., Fisher, A. N., & Ryan, M. K. (2024). *The Impact of Motherhood on Women's Career Progression: A Scoping Review of Evidence-Based Interventions. Behavioral sciences (Basel, Switzerland), 14*(4), 275. https://doi.

org/10.3390/bs14040275 Retrieved from https://pmc.ncbi.nlm.nih.gov/articles/PMC11047346/ [last accessed 08 Oct 2025]

9 Dhir, R. (2025). *How much does it cost to have a baby in America? Investopedia.* Fact checked by S. Kvilhaug. Retrieved from https://www.investopedia.com/how-much-does-it-cost-to-have-a-baby-in-america-6745508 [last accessed 08 Oct 2025]

10 Organisation for Economic Co-operation and Development (OECD). (2023). *Parental leave systems (PF2.1). OECD Family Database.* Retrieved from https://www.oecd.org/content/dam/oecd/en/data/datasets/family-database/pf2_1_parental_leave_systems.pdf [last accessed 08 Oct 2025]

11 UK Government. (2024). *Statutory maternity pay and leave: Employer guide. GOV.UK.* Retrieved from https://www.gov.uk/maternity-pay-leave/pay [last accessed 08 Oct 2025]

12 Centre for Economic Behaviour and Inequality (CEBI), University of Copenhagen. (2018). *Children and gender inequality: Evidence from Denmark. CEBI Research Report.* Retrieved from https://www.econ.ku.dk/cebi/research/2018/children-and-gender-inequality.-evidence-from-denmark/ [last accessed 08 Oct 2025]

13 Kleven, H., Landais, C. & Søgaard, J.E. (2018). *Children and gender inequality: Evidence from Denmark*, National Bureau of Economic Research. Retrieved from https://www.nber.org/papers/w24219 [last accessed: 09 Jan 2026]

14 Ibid.

15 McFall, M. R. (2024). *What is the motherhood penalty? New gender pay gap report explained. Newsweek.* Retrieved from https://www.newsweek.com/motherhood-penalty-report-gender-pay-gap-debate-fatherhood-bonus-1919965 [last accessed 08 Oct 2025]

16 World Economic Forum (WEF). (2024). *How multinationals can close parenthood wage gaps. World Economic Forum.* Retrieved from https://www.weforum.org/stories/2024/06/multinationals-can-close-parenthood-wage-gaps/ [last accessed 08 Oct 2025]

17 Office for National Statistics (ONS). (2016). *Women shoulder the responsibility of unpaid work. Office for National Statistics.* Retrieved from https://www.ons.gov.uk/employmentandlabourmarket/peopleinwork/earningsandworkinghours/articles/womenshouldertheresponsibilityofunpaidwork/2016-11-10 [last accessed 08 Oct 2025]

18 University of Bristol (2019). *Women 'less likely to progress at work' than their male counterparts following childbirth.* Retrieved from https://www.bristol.ac.uk/news/2019/october/new-mums-careers.html [last accessed 08 Oct 2025]
19 The Parenthood (2022). *Australia ranks #2 in world for most expensive childcare.* Retrieved from https://www.theparenthood.org.au/new_oecd_data [last accessed 08 Oct 2025]
20 Destatis (2022). *66% of all mothers in employment work part-time, while the relevant proportion of fathers is only 7%. Press Release.* Retrieved from https://www.destatis.de/EN/Press/2022/03/PE22_N012_12.html [last accessed 08 Oct 2025]
21 Royal London. (2024). *The pensions parenthood penalty holding women back. Royal London Press Release.* Retrieved from https://www.royallondon.com/about-us/media/media-centre/press-releases/press-releases-2024/january/the-pensions-parenthood-penalty-holding-women-back/ [last accessed 08 Oct 2025]
22 Smart, C. (2025). *Mind the Gap: Why Women Are Retiring with Less, and What You Can Do About It.* Retrieved from https://www.skyboundwealth.com/news-and-insights/mind-the-gap-why-women-are-retiring-with-less-and-what-you-can-do-about-it [last accessed 08 Oct 2025]
23 This calculation assumes that Marie is 30 years old today, and that her investments grew with the average market return of 8% per year. This is a realistic assumption, based on historic market data.
24 Whittingdale, M. & Luck, F. (2023). *'Childcare costs are pricing me out of the job market'.* Retrieved from https://www.bbc.co.uk/news/uk-england-64597414 [last accessed 08 Oct 2025]
25 Tamm, M. (2018). *Fathers' parental leave-taking, childcare involvement and mothers' labor market participation* (IZA Discussion Paper No. 11873). Institute of Labor Economics (IZA). Retrieved from https://docs.iza.org/dp11873.pdf [last accessed 08 Oct 2025]
26 Department for Business & Trade. (2023). *Shared Parental Leave: Evaluation report* (BEIS/DBT Research Paper Series No. 2023/010). Retrieved from https://assets.publishing.service.gov.uk/media/649d54be45b6a2000c3d4539/shared-parental-leave-evaluation-report-2023.pdf [last accessed 08 Oct 2025]
27 Gíslason, I. V. (2007). *Parental leave in Iceland: Bringing the fathers in.* Reykjavík: Icelandic Ministry of Welfare. Retrieved from https://www.government.is/media/velferdarraduneyti-media/media/acrobat-enskar_sidur/

Parental_Leave_in_Iceland_Bringing_the_Fathers_in.pdf [last accessed 08 Oct 2025]

28 Al-Othman, H. (2016). *Only 1% of fathers have taken advantage of shared parental leave.* Retrieved from https://www.standard.co.uk/news/uk/only-1-of-fathers-have-taken-advantage-of-shared-parental-leave-a3218091.html [last accessed 08 Oct 2025]

29 Beheshti, N. (2022). *A Father's Day question: Is better paternity leave part of the solution to burned-out working mothers? Forbes.* Retrieved from https://www.forbes.com/sites/nazbeheshti/2022/06/20/a-fathers-day-question-is-better-paternity-leave-part-of-the-solution-to-burned-out-working-mothers/ [last accessed 08 Oct 2025]

30 Brown, A. (n.d.). *What is economic abuse?* Retrieved from https://www.cabotfinancial.co.uk/money-management/understanding-debt/what-is-economic-abuse [last accessed 08 Oct 2025]

31 Oxfam GB. (n.d.). *How to make valuing all women's work a reality.* Retrieved from https://www.oxfam.org.uk/about-us/how-oxfam-changing/how-to-make-valuing-all-womens-work-a-reality/ [last accessed 08 Oct 2025]

32 Bouchet, H., Plat, A., Levréro, F., Reby, D., Patural, H., & Mathevon, N. (2020). *Baby cry recognition is independent of motherhood but improved by experience and exposure. Proceedings of the Royal Society B: Biological Sciences, 287*(1921), 2019–2499. https://doi.org/10.1098/rspb.2019.2499. Retrieved from https://pubmed.ncbi.nlm.nih.gov/32070250/ [last accessed 08 Oct 2025]

33 Consensus. (n.d.). *Do women naturally have a stronger nurturing instinct?* Retrieved from https://consensus.app/search/do-women-naturally-have-a-stronger-nurturing-insti/JI_2DsTxSJ-2BX8zefeM5g/ [last accessed 08 Oct 2025]

34 Guttmacher Institute. (2022). *Unintended Pregnancy and Abortion Worldwide* [Fact sheet]. Retrieved from https://www.guttmacher.org/fact-sheet/induced-abortion-worldwide [last accessed 08 Oct 2025]

35 For those who don't know: before having a surgical abortion, you often need to prepare the cervix by taking drugs that induce labour and stimulate contractions. These are the same drugs used for a medical abortion, which is essentially how the surgical one is started. We were sent home after the medical abortion was induced, because the doctors didn't have time anyway.

36 Foster, D. G., Biggs, M. A., Ralph, L., Gerdts, C., Roberts, S., & Glymour, M. M. (2018). *Socioeconomic Outcomes of Women Who Receive and Women Who Are Denied Wanted Abortions in the United States. American journal of public*

health, 108(3), 407–413. https://doi.org/10.2105/AJPH.2017.304247 Retrieved from https://pmc.ncbi.nlm.nih.gov/articles/PMC5803812/ [last accessed 08 Oct 2025]

37 Ludden, J. (2022). *Women who are denied abortions risk falling deeper into poverty. So do their kids.* Retrieved from https://www.npr.org/2022/05/26/1100587366/banning-abortion-roe-economic-consequences [last accessed 08 Oct 2025]

38 Iacurci, G. (2024). *Why abortion access is a personal finance issue, says demographer who studies the effects of unwanted pregnancy.* Retrieved from https://www.cnbc.com/2024/10/21/how-abortion-access-can-impact-personal-finance-turnaway-study-author.html [last accessed 08 Oct 2025]

39 Lenharo, M. (2021). *Being denied an abortion has lasting impacts on health and finances.* Retrieved from https://www.scientificamerican.com/article/being-denied-an-abortion-has-lasting-impacts-on-health-and-finances/ [last accessed 08 Oct 2025]

40 Gallen, Y., Schrøter Joensen, J., Johansen, E. R., & Veramendi, G. F. (2023). *The labor market returns to delaying pregnancy.* Becker Friedman Institute for Economics, University of Chicago. Retrieved from https://bfi.uchicago.edu/insight/research-summary/the-labor-market-returns-to-delaying-pregnancy/ [last accessed 08 Oct 2025]

41 Gallen, Y., Schrøter Joensen, J., Johansen, E. R., & Veramendi, G. F. (2023). *The labor market returns to delaying pregnancy.* Becker Friedman Institute for Economics, University of Chicago. Retrieved from https://bfi.uchicago.edu/insight/research-summary/the-labor-market-returns-to-delaying-pregnancy/ [last accessed 08 Oct 2025]]

42 NPR / KERA News (2018) *Before Roe v. Wade, the women of Jane provided abortions for the women of Chicago.* Retrieved from https://www.keranews.org/2018-01-19/before-roe-v-wade-the-women-of-jane-provided-abortions-for-the-women-of-chicago [last accessed 08 Oct 2025]

43 Haddad, L. B., & Nour, N. M. (2009). *Unsafe abortion: unnecessary maternal mortality. Reviews in obstetrics & gynecology, 2*(2), 122–126. Retrieved from https://pmc.ncbi.nlm.nih.gov/articles/PMC2709326/ [last accessed 08 Oct 2025]

44 Ibid.

45 Guttmacher Institute. (2024). *One in four U.S. women expected to have an abortion in their lifetime.* Retrieved from https://www.guttmacher.org/

news-release/2024/one-four-us-women-expected-have-abortion-their-lifetime [last accessed 08 Oct 2025]
46 University of Oxford Faculty of Law. (2017). *1 in 3 women in the UK will have an abortion – so why is it so secret?* Retrieved from https://www.law.ox.ac.uk/news/2017-10-12-1-3-women-uk-will-have-abortion-so-why-it-so-secret [last accessed 08 Oct 2025]
47 Information (Denmark). (2003). *Rapport underkender abort-myter.* Retrieved from https://www.information.dk/2003/11/rapport-underkender-abort-myter [last accessed 08 Oct 2025]
48 Office for National Statistics (ONS). (2023). *Families and households in the UK: 2023.* Retrieved from https://www.ons.gov.uk/peoplepopulationandcommunity/birthsdeathsandmarriages/families/bulletins/familiesandhouseholds/2023 [last accessed 08 Oct 2025]

The Secret to Success? Having a Penis

1 Gulliver-Needham, E. (2024). *IWD: There are more FTSE 100 CEOs with these two names than women. City AM.* Retrieved from https://www.cityam.com/iwd-there-are-more-ftse-100-ceos-with-these-two-names-than-women/ [last accessed 08 Oct 2025]
2 Pompeu Fabra University (UPF). (2019). *Women are 30% less likely to be considered for a hiring process than men.* Retrieved from https://www.upf.edu/en/recercaupf/-/asset_publisher/RVNxhLpxnc9g/content/id/223062374/maximized [last accessed 08 Oct 2025]
3 Textio. (2024). *Language Bias in Performance Feedback 2024. Who gets the most useless feedback at work?* Retrieved from https://textio.com/feedback-bias-2024 [last accessed 08 Oct 2025]
4 BBC News. (2020). *Firms with more female executives 'perform better.'* Retrieved from https://www.bbc.com/news/business-53548704 [last accessed 08 Oct 2025]
5 Kanze, D., Huang, L., Conley, M. A., & Higgins, E. T. (2017). *Male and female entrepreneurs get asked different questions by VCs—and it affects how much funding they get. Harvard Business Review.* Retrieved from https://hbr.org/2017/06/male-and-female-entrepreneurs-get-asked-different-questions-by-vcs-and-it-affects-how-much-funding-they-get [last accessed 08 Oct 2025]
6 Boston Consulting Group (BCG). (2018). *Why women-owned startups are a*

better bet. Retrieved from https://www.bcg.com/publications/2018/why-women-owned-startups-are-better-bet [last accessed 08 Oct 2025]

7 Lord, A. (2017). *Antibodies are a girl's best friend.* Retrieved from https://americanhistory.si.edu/explore/stories/antibodies-are-girls-best-friend [last accessed 10 Nov 2025]

8 Future Market Insights Inc. (2025). *At-Home Pregnancy Testing Market Size and Share Forecast Outlook (2025 to 2035).* Retrieved from https://www.futuremarketinsights.com/reports/at-home-pregnancy-testing-market [last accessed 10 Nov 2025]

9 Equal Pay Today. (2025). *Gender pay gap statistics.* Retrieved from https://www.equalpaytoday.org/gender-pay-gap-statistics/ [last accessed 08 Oct 2025]

10 Office for National Statistics (ONS). (2024). *Gender pay gap in the UK: 2024.* Retrieved from https://www.ons.gov.uk/employmentandlabourmarket/peopleinwork/earningsandworkinghours/bulletins/genderpaygapintheuk/2024 [last accessed 08 Oct 2025]

11 UK Government. (2024). *UK businesses lead the way with record numbers of female leaders.* Retrieved from https://www.gov.uk/government/news/uk-businesses-lead-the-way-with-record-numbers-of-female-leaders [last accessed 08 Oct 2025]

12 Fast Company. (2020). *The 'Peter Problem': Study finds more FTSE CEOs named Peter than women.* Retrieved from https://www.fastcompany.com/90534066/what-is-a-peter-problem-jaw-dropping-study-of-u-k-ceos-reveals-more-named-peter-than-women [last accessed 08 Oct 2025]

13 Novotney, A. (2023). *Women leaders make work better. Here's the science behind how to promote them.* American Psychological Association (APA). Retrieved from https://www.apa.org/topics/women-girls/female-leaders-make-work-better [last accessed 08 Oct 2025]

14 Theus, D. (2024). *Are Women Better Leaders Than Men? Exploring the Leadership Gender Gap.* Retrieved from https://inpowercoaching.com/women-better-leaders/ [last accessed 08 Oct 2025]

15 Vestpod. (2025). *Women are outperforming in investing.* Retrieved from https://www.vestpod.com/news/women-are-outperforming-in-investing [last accessed 08 Oct 2025]

16 Boston Consulting Group (BCG). (2018). *Why women-owned startups are a better bet.* Retrieved from https://www.bcg.com/publications/2018/why-women-owned-startups-are-better-bet [last accessed 08 Oct 2025]

17 BBC News. (2020). *Firms with more female executives 'perform better.'* Retrieved from https://www.bbc.com/news/business-53548704 [last accessed 08 Oct 2025]

18 BBC News. (2020). *Firms with more female executives 'perform better.'* Retrieved from https://www.bbc.com/news/business-53548704 [last accessed 08 Oct 2025]

19 World Economic Forum. (2026). *The Global Gender Parity Sprint to 2030: How we are scaling parity and opportunity for 1.5 million women.* Retrieved from https://www.weforum.org/impact/global-gender-parity-sprint-to-2030-scaling-parity-and-opportunity-for-women/ [last accessed: 06 Feb 2026]

20 Pompeu Fabra University (UPF). (2019). *Women are 30% less likely to be considered for a hiring process than men.* Retrieved from https://www.upf.edu/en/recercaupf/-/asset_publisher/RVNxhLpxnc9g/content/id/223062374/maximized [last accessed 08 Oct 2025]

21 Wilson, K. & Caliskan, A. (2025). *Gender, race, and intersectional bias in AI résumé screening via language model retrieval.* Brookings Institution. Retrieved from https://www.brookings.edu/articles/gender-race-and-intersectional-bias-in-ai-resume-screening-via-language-model-retrieval/ [last accessed 08 Oct 2025]

22 Moss-Racusin, C.A., Dovidio, J.F. Brescoll, V.L., Graham M.J. & Handelsman, J. (2012). *Science faculty's subtle gender biases favor male students. Proc. Natl. Acad. Sci.*, 109 (41), 16474–16479, *https://doi.org/10.1073/pnas.1211286109* [last accessed: 06 Feb 2026]

23 Cooper, M. (2013). *For women leaders, likability and success hardly go hand in hand. Harvard Business Review.* Retrieved from https://hbr.org/2013/04/for-women-leaders-likability-a [last accessed 08 Oct 2025]

24 Kong, M. (2022). *On Heidis, Howards, and Hierarchies: Gender Gap in Medicine. Frontiers in pediatrics, 10,* 901297. https://doi.org/10.3389/fped.2022.901297 Retrieved from https://pmc.ncbi.nlm.nih.gov/articles/PMC9086970/ [last accessed 08 Oct 2025]

25 Kolmetz, K. (n.d.). *Heidi vs. Howard: A case study in gender bias.* Retrieved from https://toolbox.humandeluxe.com/heidi-vs-howard [last accessed 08 Oct 2025]

26 Textio. (2024). *Language Bias in Performance Feedback 2024. Who gets the most useless feedback at work?* Retrieved from https://textio.com/feedback-bias-2024 [last accessed 08 Oct 2025]

27 Burleigh, E. (2024, August 8). *About 76% of top-performing women encounter negative feedback compared to just 2% of men—and it's making them want to quit. Fortune.* Retrieved from https://fortune.com/2024/08/08/most-high-performing-women-recieve-negative-feedback-quit-jobs/ [last accessed 08 Oct 2025]
28 Blanding, M. (2018, December 17). *Women receive harsher punishment at work than men.* Harvard Business School. Retrieved from https://www.library.hbs.edu/working-knowledge/women-receive-harsher-punishment-at-work-than-men [last accessed 08 Oct 2025]
29 Jackson, I. (2025). *Seven in ten women experience imposter syndrome at work, research finds. People Management.* Retrieved from https://www.peoplemanagement.co.uk/article/1919598/exclusive-seven-10-women-experience-imposter-syndrome-work-research-finds [last accessed 08 Oct 2025]
30 Bradshaw, M. (2025). *The invisible load: Non-Promotable tasks and the burden on women – raft cares.* Retrieved from https://www.raftcares.org/resources/community-blog/non-promotable-task/ [last accessed 08 Oct 2025]
31 McKinsey & Company & LeanIn.Org. (2024). *Women in the workplace 2024.* Retrieved from https://www.mckinsey.com/featured-insights/diversity-and-inclusion/women-in-the-workplace [last accessed 08 Oct 2025]
32 United Nations (UN). (n.d.). *International Equal Pay Day.* Retrieved from https://www.un.org/en/observances/equal-pay-day [last accessed 08 Oct 2025]
33 University College London (UCL). (2024). *Millennial women paid less than male colleagues in similar jobs, study finds.* Retrieved from https://www.ucl.ac.uk/news/2024/dec/millennial-women-paid-less-male-colleagues-similar-jobs [last accessed 08 Oct 2025]
34 Miller, C. (2016). *As women take over a male-dominated field, the pay drops. The New York Times.* Retrieved from https://www.nytimes.com/2016/03/20/upshot/as-women-take-over-a-male-dominated-field-the-pay-drops.html [last accessed 08 Oct 2025]
35 Levanon, A., England, P., & Allison, P. (2009). *Occupational Feminization and Pay: Assessing Causal Dynamics Using 1950–2000 U.S. Census Data. Social Forces,* Volume 88, Issue 2, December 2009, pp. 865–891, https://doi.org/10.1353/sof.0.0264, Retrieved from https://academic.oup.com/sf/article-abstract/88/2/865/2235342 [last accessed 08 Oct 2025]
36 Harris, J. (2021). *Do wages fall when women enter an occupation?* Retrieved

from https://www.sciencedirect.com/science/article/abs/pii/S0927537121001378 [last accessed 08 Oct 2025]

37 Parkhurst, E. (2024). *Women don't choose lower-pay jobs — wages drop when women enter an industry.* Retrieved from https://beformidable.com/p/women-dont-choose-lower-pay-jobs-gender-wage-gap [last accessed 08 Oct 2025]

38 PayScale. (n.d.). *When an occupation becomes female-dominated, pay declines.* Retrieved from https://www.payscale.com/career-advice/when-an-occupation-becomes-female-dominated-pay-declines [last accessed 08 Oct 2025]

39 Shackleton, L. (2016). *As women enter an occupation, average pay falls — sexism? No, just supply and demand.* Institute of Economic Affairs (IEA). Retrieved from https://iea.org.uk/blog/as-women-enter-an-occupation-average-pay-falls-sexism-no-just-supply-and-demand [last accessed 08 Oct 2025]

40 Academy of Management (AOM). (2024). *Axios: Women MBAs are asking for higher pay — but still earning less.* Retrieved from https://www.aom.org/news/axios-women-mbas-are-asking-for-higher-pay-but-still-earning-less/ [last accessed 08 Oct 2025]

41 Kray, L. J., Kennedy, J. A., & Lee, M. (2023). *Now, Women Do Ask: A Call to Update Beliefs about the Gender Pay Gap. Academy of Management Discoveries, 10*(1), 11–37. https://doi.org/10.5465/amd.2022.0021 Retrieved from https://journals.aom.org/doi/abs/10.5465/amd.2022.0021 [last accessed 08 Oct 2025]

42 Elsesser, K. (2023). *Women more likely to negotiate salaries but still earn less than men, research says. Forbes.* Retrieved from https://www.forbes.com/sites/kimelsesser/2023/11/02/women-more-likely-to-negotiate-salaries-but-still-earn-less-than-men-research-says/ [last accessed 08 Oct 2025]

43 University of Southern California. (2023, September 19). *Are women worse than men at salary negotiation? USC Today.* Retrieved from https://today.usc.edu/women-men-salary-negotiation-virtual-agents-usc-research/ [last accessed 08 Oct 2025]

44 Odell, J. (2024). *Supporting female founders could unlock billions in growth.* UK Business Angels Association (UKBAA). Retrieved from https://ukbaa.org.uk/blog/2024/12/05/supporting-female-founders-could-unlock-billions-in-growth/ [last accessed 08 Oct 2025]

45 Shunina, D. (2023). *Female founders received only 2% of total capital in 2022, according to Pitchbook report. Forbes.* Retrieved from https://www.forbes.com/sites/dariashunina/2023/12/11/female-founders-received-only-2-of-total-capital-in-2023-according-to-pitchbook-report/ [last accessed 08 Oct 2025]

46 Boston Consulting Group (BCG). (2018). *Why women-owned startups are a better bet.* Retrieved from https://www.bcg.com/publications/2018/why-women-owned-startups-are-better-bet [last accessed 08 Oct 2025]
47 Lewin, A. (2022). *Only 15% of VC general partners in Europe are women. Sifted.* Retrieved from https://sifted.eu/articles/vc-general-partners-europe [last accessed 08 Oct 2025]
48 Brooks, A. W., et al. (2014). *Investors prefer entrepreneurial ventures pitched by attractive men. Proceedings of the National Academy of Sciences of the United States of America (PNAS), 111*(12), 4427–4431. Retrieved from https://gap.hks.harvard.edu/investors-prefer-entrepreneurial-ventures-pitched-attractive-men [last accessed 08 Oct 2025]
49 Kanze, D., Huang, L., Conley, M. A., & Higgins, E. T. (2017). *Male and female entrepreneurs get asked different questions by VCs — and it affects how much funding they get. Harvard Business Review.* Retrieved from https://hbr.org/2017/06/male-and-female-entrepreneurs-get-asked-different-questions-by-vcs-and-it-affects-how-much-funding-they-get [last accessed 08 Oct 2025]
50 Dealroom & HSBC Innovation Banking. (2025). *UK Q4 2024–2025 Innovation Update.* Retrieved from https://dealroom.co/uploaded/2025/01/UK-Q4-2024-2025-Innovation-Update-Dealroom-x-HSBC-Innovation-Banking.pdf [last accessed 08 Oct 2025]
51 United Nations Development Programme (UNDP). (2020). *Women's participation in decision-making: Why it matters.* Retrieved from https://www.undp.org/ghana/news/womens-participation-decision-making-why-it-matters [last accessed 08 Oct 2025]
52 International Labour Organization (ILO). (2019). *Women in business and management: The business case for change.* Retrieved from https://www.ilo.org/sites/default/files/wcmsp5/groups/public/@dgreports/@dcomm/@publ/documents/publication/wcms_700953.pdf [last accessed 08 Oct 2025]
53 GWL Voices. (2024). *The imperative of gender equality in multilateral decision-making.* Retrieved from https://www.gwlvoices.org/actions/the-imperative-of-gender-equality-in-multilateral-decision-making [last accessed 08 Oct 2025]

Menopause: Hot Flush, Cold Reality

1 UK House of Commons Library. (2021). *Support for people experiencing*

menopausal symptoms. Research Briefing CDP-2021-0078. Retrieved from https://commonslibrary.parliament.uk/research-briefings/cdp-2021-0078/ [last accessed 08 Oct 2025]

2 New Natural Business. (n.d.). *Menopausal women being prescribed 'inappropriate' antidepressants.* Retrieved from https://www.newnaturalbusiness.co.uk/insights-menopausal-women [last accessed 08 Oct 2025]

3 Chartered Institute of Personnel and Development (CIPD). (2019). *Majority of working women experiencing the menopause say it has a negative impact on them at work.* Retrieved from https://www.cipd.org/en/about/press-releases/menopause-at-work/ [last accessed 08 Oct 2025]

4 UK Government. (2024). *Shattering the silence about menopause: 12-month progress report.* Retrieved from https://www.gov.uk/government/publications/shattering-the-silence-about-menopause-12-month-progress-report/shattering-the-silence-about-menopause-12-month-progress-report [last accessed 08 Oct 2025]

5 Balance Menopause. (2024). *Menopause puts the final nail in the marriage coffin, study finds.* Retrieved from https://www.balance-menopause.com/news/menopause-puts-final-nail-in-marriage-coffin/ [last accessed 08 Oct 2025]

6 UK House of Commons Library. (2021). *Support for people experiencing menopausal symptoms. Research Briefing CDP-2021-0078.* Retrieved from https://commonslibrary.parliament.uk/research-briefings/cdp-2021-0078/ [last accessed 08 Oct 2025]

7 Newson, L. (2025). *Antidepressants and menopause: What you need to know. Dr. Louise Newson Clinic.* Retrieved from https://www.drlouisenewson.co.uk/knowledge/antidepressants-and-menopause [last accessed 08 Oct 2025]

8 New Natural Business. (n.d.). *Menopausal women being prescribed 'inappropriate' antidepressants.* Retrieved from https://www.newnaturalbusiness.co.uk/insights-menopausal-women [last accessed 08 Oct 2025]

9 National Health Service (NHS). (n.d). *About hormone replacement therapy (HRT).* Retrieved from https://www.nhs.uk/medicines/hormone-replacement-therapy-hrt/about-hormone-replacement-therapy-hrt/ [last accessed 08 Oct 2025]

10 Hodis, H. N., & Mack, W. J. (2022). *Menopausal Hormone Replacement Therapy and Reduction of All-Cause Mortality and Cardiovascular Disease: It Is About Time and Timing. Cancer journal (Sudbury, Mass.), 28*(3), 208–223. https://doi.org/10.1097/PPO.0000000000000591 Retrieved from https://pmc.ncbi.nlm.nih.gov/articles/PMC9178928/ [last accessed 08 Oct 2025]

11 National Health Service (NHS). (n.d). *About hormone replacement therapy (HRT).* Retrieved from https://www.nhs.uk/medicines/hormone-replacement-therapy-hrt/about-hormone-replacement-therapy-hrt/ [last accessed 08 Oct 2025]

12 Mehta, J., Kling, J. M., & Manson, J. E. (2021). *Risks, Benefits, and Treatment Modalities of Menopausal Hormone Therapy: Current Concepts. Frontiers in endocrinology, 12*, 564781. https://doi.org/10.3389/fendo.2021.564781 Retrieved from https://pmc.ncbi.nlm.nih.gov/articles/PMC8034540/ [last accessed 08 Oct 2025]

13 Menopause Support. (2021). *Survey – Menopause Training in Medical Schools.* Retrieved from https://menopausesupport.co.uk/?p=14434 [last accessed 08 Oct 2025]

14 Menopause Support. (2021). *Menopause support survey reveals shocking disparity in menopause training in medical schools* [PDF]. Retrieved from https://menopausesupport.co.uk/wp-content/uploads/2021/05/Web-info-Shocking-Disparity-in-Menopause-Training-in-Medical-Schools-1.pdf [last accessed 08 Oct 2025]

15 Price, R. (2021). *Wicked or wise? Menopausal women in popular history. Epoch Magazine.* Retrieved from https://www.epoch-magazine.com/post/wicked-or-wise-menopausal-women-in-popular-history [last accessed 08 Oct 2025]

16 Smellie, A. (2022). *Misogyny & the menopause: A brief history.* Retrieved from https://www.panmacmillan.com/blogs/lifestyle-wellbeing/menopause-history-alice-smellie [last accessed 08 Oct 2025]

17 Howes, H. (2014). *Watery offerings: Women and water in the Middle Ages. Emotions Blog.* Retrieved from https://emotionsblog.history.qmul.ac.uk/2014/05/watery-offerings-women-and-water-in-the-middle-ages/ [last accessed 08 Oct 2025]

18 Price, R. (2021). *Wicked or wise? Menopausal women in popular history. Epoch Magazine.* Retrieved from https://www.epoch-magazine.com/post/wicked-or-wise-menopausal-women-in-popular-history [last accessed 08 Oct 2025]

19 UK Parliament. (2023). *Menopause and the workplace: First report of session 2022–23.* Retrieved from https://publications.parliament.uk/pa/cm5803/cmselect/cmwomeq/91/report.html [last accessed 08 Oct 2025]

20 Tatum, M. (2024). *Without support, many menopausal workers are quitting their jobs.* BBC Worklife. Retrieved from https://www.bbc.com/worklife/article/20240408-menopause-women-job-quits [last accessed 08 Oct 2025]

21 UK Government. (2024). *Shattering the silence about menopause: 12-month progress report.* Retrieved from https://www.gov.uk/government/publications/shattering-the-silence-about-menopause-12-month-progress-report/shattering-the-silence-about-menopause-12-month-progress-report [last accessed 08 Oct 2025]

22 Chartered Institute of Personnel and Development (CIPD). (2019). *Majority of working women experiencing the menopause say it has a negative impact on them at work.* Retrieved from https://www.cipd.org/en/about/press-releases/menopause-at-work/ [last accessed 08 Oct 2025]

23 Chartered Institute of Personnel and Development (CIPD). (2023). *Over a quarter of women say menopause has had a negative impact on their career progression, new CIPD research finds.* Retrieved from https://www.cipd.org/en/about/press-releases/quarter-of-women-menopause-negative-impact-on-career/ [last accessed 08 Oct 2025]

24 UK Government. (2024). *Menopause and workplace productivity.* Retrieved from https://www.gov.uk/government/publications/menopause-and-workplace-productivity/menopause-and-workplace-productivity [last accessed 08 Oct 2025]

25 Elkins, K. (2018). *Here's the age at which you'll earn the most in your career. CNBC.* Retrieved from https://www.cnbc.com/2018/11/02/the-age-at-which-youll-earn-the-most-money-in-your-career.html [last accessed 08 Oct 2025]

26 PayScale. (2024). *Earnings Peak at Different Ages for Different Demographic Groups.* Retrieved from https://www.payscale.com/research-and-insights/peak-earnings [last accessed 08 Oct 2025]

27 Andrieux, J. P. (2021). *IFS: Most pension contributions come after age 45. Money Marketing.* Retrieved from https://www.moneymarketing.co.uk/news/ifs-most-pension-contributions-come-after-age-45/ [last accessed 08 Oct 2025]

28 These numbers assume an average salary and 8% contribution of earnings into a pension from the age of 25 without any breaks.

29 Nunn, B. (2024). *Menopause: The hidden tax on your pension. Fidelity Retirement.* Retrieved from https://retirement.fidelity.co.uk/news-insights/financial-wellness/financial-wellness/menopause-the-hidden-tax-on-your-pension/ [last accessed 08 Oct 2025]

30 Abode Financial. (2025). *Closing the gender pension gap: Practical steps for women.* Retrieved from https://abodefinancial.co.uk/blog/gender-pension-gap/ [last accessed 08 Oct 2025]

31 Actuarial Post. (n.d.). *Men have nearly twice as much pension wealth as women.* Retrieved from https://www.actuarialpost.co.uk/article/men-have-nearly-twice-as-much-pension-wealth-as-women-24516.htm [last accessed 08 Oct 2025]
32 Actuarial Post. (n.d.). *Men have nearly twice as much pension wealth as women.* Retrieved from https://www.actuarialpost.co.uk/article/men-have-nearly-twice-as-much-pension-wealth-as-women-24516.htm [last accessed 15 Dec 2025]
33 Grand View Research. (2024). *Menopause market size, share & trends analysis report.* Retrieved from https://www.grandviewresearch.com/industry-analysis/menopause-market [last accessed 08 Oct 2025]
34 International Monetary Fund (IMF). (2025). *Country profile: Armenia.* Retrieved from https://www.imf.org/external/datamapper/profile/ARM [last accessed 08 Oct 2025]
35 National Health Service Business Services Authority (NHSBSA). (2024). *NHS Hormone Replacement Therapy prescription prepayment certificate (HRT PPC).* Retrieved from https://www.nhsbsa.nhs.uk/help-nhs-prescription-costs/nhs-hormone-replacement-therapy-prescription-prepayment-certificate-hrt-ppc [last accessed 08 Oct 2025]
36 Jaffe, L. (2023). *The hidden costs of menopause: How it affects workers and what employers can do to help.* Retrieved from https://www.fromdayone.com/stories/2023/10/5/the-hidden-costs-of-menopause-how-it-affects-workersand-what-employers-can-do-to-help [last accessed 08 Oct 2025]
37 Notarantonio, L. (2025). *Expert Shares Why Japanese Women Have Less Severe Menopause Symptoms.* Retrieved from https://www.newsweek.com/why-japanese-women-less-severe-menopause-symptoms-2042913 [last accessed 08 Oct 2025]
38 Lincoln Nichols, D. (2024). *Six countries offering annual menopause leave.* Retrieved from https://dixielincolnnichols.com/6-countries-offering-annual-menopause-leave/ [last accessed 08 Oct 2025]
39 Balance Menopause. (2024). *Menopause puts the final nail in the marriage coffin, study finds.* Retrieved from https://www.balance-menopause.com/news/menopause-puts-final-nail-in-marriage-coffin/ [last accessed 08 Oct 2025]
40 Yurday, E. (2024). *Divorce statistics UK 2023.* Retrieved from https://www.nimblefins.co.uk/divorce-statistics-uk [last accessed 08 Oct 2025]
41 Balance Menopause. (2024). *Menopause puts the final nail in the marriage

coffin, study finds. Retrieved from https://www.balance-menopause.com/news/menopause-puts-final-nail-in-marriage-coffin/ [last accessed 08 Oct 2025]
42 Lin, I. F., & Brown, S. L. (2021). *The Economic Consequences of Gray Divorce for Women and Men. The journals of gerontology. Series B, Psychological sciences and social sciences, 76*(10), 2073–2085. https://doi.org/10.1093/geronb/gbaa157 Retrieved from https://pmc.ncbi.nlm.nih.gov/articles/PMC8599059/ [last accessed 08 Oct 2025]
43 Mercy Foundation. (n.d.). *Older women and homelessness.* Retrieved from https://www.mercyfoundation.com.au/our-focus/ending-homelessness/older-women-and-homelessness/ [last accessed 08 Oct 2025]
44 Committee on Women and Equalities. (2025). *Older Women, Poverty and Financial Insecurity in the UK. Written evidence submitted to the UK Parliament (MEN0045).* Retrieved from https://committees.parliament.uk/writtenevidence/133425/pdf/ [last accessed 08 Oct 2025]
45 Lin, I. F., & Brown, S. L. (2021). *The Economic Consequences of Gray Divorce for Women and Men. The journals of gerontology. Series B, Psychological sciences and social sciences, 76*(10), 2073–2085. https://doi.org/10.1093/geronb/gbaa157 Retrieved from https://pmc.ncbi.nlm.nih.gov/articles/PMC8599059/ [last accessed 08 Oct 2025]
46 The White House. (2024). *Economic security of older women.* Retrieved from https://bidenwhitehouse.archives.gov/cea/written-materials/2024/09/20/economic-security-of-older-women/ [last accessed 08 Oct 2025]
47 The Australian Government (2025). Australian Government response to the Senate Community Affairs References Committee report: Issues related to menopause and perimenopause. Retrieved from https://www.health.gov.au/sites/default/files/2025-02/government-response-to-inquiry-issues-related-to-menopause-and-perimenopause.pdf [last accessed 08 Oct 2025]
48 The Australian Government Department of Health (2025). National Women's Health Strategy 2020-2030. https://www.health.gov.au/sites/default/files/documents/2021/05/national-women-s-health-strategy-2020-2030_0.pdf

All the Single Ladies

1 Morgan Stanley. (2019). *Rise of the SHEconomy.* Retrieved from https://www.morganstanley.com/ideas/womens-impact-on-the-economy [last accessed 09 Oct 2025]

2 Cain, S. (2019). *Women are happier without children or a spouse, says happiness expert. Guardian.* Retrieved from https://www.theguardian.com/lifeandstyle/2019/may/25/women-happier-without-children-or-a-spouse-happiness-expert [last accessed 09 Oct 2025]

3 Sørensen, L. (2025). *Statistics reveal 60% rise in solo mums by choice in the UK.* European Sperm Bank. Retrieved from https://www.europeanspermbank.com/blog-en-int/blog-posts/dramatic-rise-in-women-choosing-to-be-solo-mums-by-choice [last accessed 09 Oct 2025]

4 Golombok, S., Zadeh, S., Imrie, S., Smith, V., & Freeman, T. (2016). Single mothers by choice: Mother-child relationships and children's psychological adjustment. *Journal of family psychology: JFP: journal of the Division of Family Psychology of the American Psychological Association (Division 43), 30*(4), 409–418. https://doi.org/10.1037/fam0000188 Retrieved from https://pmc.ncbi.nlm.nih.gov/articles/PMC4886836/ [last accessed 09 Oct 2025]

5 Munsch, L. (2015) *Her Support, His Support: Money, Masculinity, and Marital Infidelity. American Sociological Review.* Retrieved from https://www.asanet.org/wp-content/uploads/savvy/journals/CS/Jun15ASRFeature.pdf [last accessed 09 Oct 2025]

6 American Sociological Association. (2010). *Men more likely to cheat if they are economically dependent on their female partners, study finds. ScienceDaily.* Retrieved from www.sciencedaily.com/releases/2010/08/100816095617.htm [last accessed 09 Oct 2025]

7 Bhattarai, A. (2023). *Single women take an outsize role in the workforce — and the economy.* Retrieved from https://fortune.com/2023/03/22/single-unmarried-women-fast-growing-workforce/ [last accessed 09 Oct 2025]

8 Morgan Stanley. (2019). *Rise of the SHEconomy.* Retrieved from https://www.morganstanley.com/ideas/womens-impact-on-the-economy [last accessed 09 Oct 2025]

9 Cain, S. (2019). *Women are happier without children or a spouse, says happiness expert. Guardian.* Retrieved from https://www.theguardian.com/lifeandstyle/2019/may/25/women-happier-without-children-or-a-spouse-happiness-expert [last accessed 09 Oct 2025]

10 Bhattarai, A. (2023). *Single women take an outsize role in the workforce — and the economy.* Retrieved from https://fortune.com/2023/03/22/single-unmarried-women-fast-growing-workforce/ [last accessed 09 Oct 2025]

11 Statista. (2025). *Completion rates among bachelor students 2020, by gender.*

Retrieved from https://www.statista.com/statistics/1346409/completion-rate-higher-education-oecd-gender/ [last accessed 09 Oct 2025]

12 Morgan Stanley. (2019). *Rise of the SHEconomy.* Retrieved from https://www.morganstanley.com/ideas/womens-impact-on-the-economy [last accessed 09 Oct 2025]

13 Davis, K. (2019). *20 facts and figures to know when marketing to women. Forbes.* Retrieved from https://www.forbes.com/sites/forbescontentmarketing/2019/05/13/20-facts-and-figures-to-know-when-marketing-to-women/ [last accessed 09 Oct 2025]

14 Currie, M. (2023). *Is the future of wealth female?* Hargreaves Lansdown. Retrieved from https://www.hl.co.uk/news/is-the-future-of-wealth-female [last accessed 09 Oct 2025]

15 ABC News. (2010). *Reverse Gender Gap: Study Says Young, Childless Women Earn More Than Men.* Retrieved from https://abcnews.go.com/WN/reverse-gender-gap-study-young-childless-women-earn/story?id=11538401 [last accessed 09 Oct 2025]

16 Goldstein, J. (2010). *Young, Single & Childless: Women Who Earn More Than Men.* NPR. Retrieved from https://www.npr.org/sections/money/2010/09/01/129581758/ [last accessed 09 Oct 2025]

17 Fry, R. (2022). *Young women are out-earning young men in several U.S. cities.* Pew Research Center. Retrieved from https://www.pewresearch.org/short-reads/2022/03/28/young-women-are-out-earning-young-men-in-several-u-s-cities/ [last accessed 09 Oct 2025]

18 Spector, N. (2020). *Single women own more homes than single men. Here's what they're doing differently.* NBC News. Retrieved from https://www.nbcnews.com/better/lifestyle/single-women-own-more-homes-single-men-here-s-what-ncna1134926 [last accessed 09 Oct 2025]

19 Colley, N. (2023). *More Single Women Are Working Than Ever, But Their Pay Gap Has Grown, Report Shows.* Retrieved from https://www.forbes.com/sites/nataliecolley/2023/04/17/single-women-face-steepest-gender-wealth-penalty-according-to-report/ [last accessed 09 Oct 2025]

20 Niimi, Y. (2022). *Are married women really wealthier than unmarried women? Demography, 59*(2), 461–484. Duke University Press. Retrieved from https://read.dukeupress.edu/demography/article/59/2/461/294245/Are-Married-Women-Really-Wealthier-Than-Unmarried [last accessed 09 Oct 2025]

21 Niimi, Y. (2022). *Are married women really wealthier than unmarried women?*

Demography, 59(2), 461–484. Duke University Press. Retrieved from https://read.dukeupress.edu/demography/article/59/2/461/294245/Are-Married-Women-Really-Wealthier-Than-Unmarried [last accessed 09 Oct 2025]

22 Brown, A. (2020). *A profile of single Americans.* Pew Research Center. Retrieved from https://www.pewresearch.org/social-trends/2020/08/20/a-profile-of-single-americans/ [last accessed 09 Oct 2025]

23 Fry, R., Aragão, C., Hurst, K. & Parker, K. (2023). *In a growing share of U.S. marriages, husbands and wives earn about the same.* Retrieved from https://www.pewresearch.org/social-trends/2023/04/13/in-a-growing-share-of-u-s-marriages-husbands-and-wives-earn-about-the-same/ [last accessed 09 Oct 2025]

24 Adamczyk, A. (2023). *Only half of the women who are out-earning their husbands are taking the lead on household expenses, UBS says. Fortune.* Retrieved from https://fortune.com/2023/06/13/female-breadwinners-rising-ubs-report/ [last accessed 09 Oct 2025]

25 Lines, C. (2020). *Men feel happy if they earn more than their wives, study shows.* Retrieved from https://www.citystgeorges.ac.uk/news-and-events/news/2020/11/men-feel-happy-if-they-earn-more-than-their-wives-study-shows [last accessed 09 Oct 2025]

26 Munsch, L. (2015). *Her Support, His Support: Money, Masculinity, and Marital Infidelity. American Sociological Review.* Retrieved from https://www.asanet.org/wp-content/uploads/savvy/journals/CS/Jun15ASRFeature.pdf [last accessed 09 Oct 2025]

27 American Sociological Association. (2010). *Men more likely to cheat if they are economically dependent on their female partners, study finds. ScienceDaily.* Retrieved from www.sciencedaily.com/releases/2010/08/100816095617.htm [last accessed 09 Oct 2025]

28 World Economic Forum. (2022). *What does the global decline of the fertility rate look like?* Retrieved from https://www.weforum.org/stories/2022/06/global-decline-of-fertility-rates-visualised/ [last accessed 09 Oct 2025]

29 Dattani, S., Rodés-Guirao, L., & Roser, M. (2025, February 24). *Fertility rate.* Our World in Data. Retrieved from https://ourworldindata.org/fertility-rate [last accessed 09 Oct 2025]

30 Sørensen, L. (2025). *Statistics reveal 60% rise in solo mums by choice in the UK.* European Sperm Bank. Retrieved from https://www.europeanspermbank.com/blog-en-int/blog-posts/dramatic-rise-in-women-choosing-to-be-solo-mums-by-choice [last accessed 09 Oct 2025]

31 Tomasino, J. (2023). *IVF cost: Understanding the expenses of in vitro fertilization.* Retrieved from https://www.get-carrot.com/blog/ivf-cost-understanding-the-expenses-of-in-vitro-fertilization [last accessed 09 Oct 2025]

32 AdoptUSKids. (n.d.). *What is the cost of adoption from foster care?* Retrieved from https://adoptuskids.org/adoption-and-foster-care/overview/what-does-it-cost [last accessed 09 Oct 2025]

33 LV=. (2025). *How much will it cost to raise a child in 2025?* Retrieved from https://www.lv.com/life-insurance/articles/cost-of-raising-a-child [last accessed 09 Oct 2025]

34 Sheldon, J. (2025). *Women's financial freedom: How money has changed in 50 years.* MoneyWeek. Retrieved from https://moneyweek.com/personal-finance/women-money-changes-gender-gap [last accessed 09 Oct 2025]

35 Science Daily. (2017). *Children in single-mother-by-choice families do just as well as those in two-parent families.* Retrieved from https://www.sciencedaily.com/releases/2017/07/170705095332.htm [last accessed 09 Oct 2025]

36 Sørensen, L. (2025). *Statistics reveal 60% rise in solo mums by choice in the UK.* European Sperm Bank. Retrieved from https://www.europeanspermbank.com/blog-en-int/blog-posts/dramatic-rise-in-women-choosing-to-be-solo-mums-by-choice [last accessed 09 Oct 2025]

37 Golombok, S., Zadeh, S., Imrie, S., Smith, V., & Freeman, T. (2016). *Single mothers by choice: Mother-child relationships and children's psychological adjustment. Journal of family psychology: JFP: journal of the Division of Family Psychology of the American Psychological Association (Division 43), 30*(4), 409–418. https://doi.org/10.1037/fam0000188 Retrieved from https://pmc.ncbi.nlm.nih.gov/articles/PMC4886836/ [last accessed 09 Oct 2025]

38 Ibid.

39 Kassam, A. (2024). *'Lens of a singleton': Belgian council to focus on those who live alone. Guardian.* Retrieved from https://www.theguardian.com/world/2024/feb/14/lens-singleton-belgian-council-focus-live-alone [last accessed 09 Oct 2025]

Masculinity Meltdown

1 UK Parliament Education Committee. (2024). *Why do boys lag behind girls at all ages of education? MPs to investigate.* Retrieved from https://committees.parliament.uk/committee/203/education-committee/news/200976/

why-do-boys-lag-behind-girls-at-all-ages-of-education-mps-to-investigate/ [last accessed 09 Oct 2025]

2 Hillman, N. & Brooks, M. (2025). *Boys will be boys: The educational underachievement of boys and young men.* Higher Education Policy Institute (HEPI). Retrieved from https://www.hepi.ac.uk/wp-content/uploads/2025/03/Boys-will-be-boys-The-educational-underachievement-of-boys-and-young-men.pdf [last accessed 09 Oct 2025]

3 Bloomberg News. (2025). *Data reveals how men are falling behind in school and work.* Retrieved from https://www.bloomberg.com/news/features/2025-04-21/data-reveals-how-men-are-falling-behind-in-school-and-work? [last accessed 09 Oct 2025]

4 Cappelen, A. W., Falch, R., & Tungodden, B. (2025). *Experimental evidence on the acceptance of males falling behind. Journal of the European Economic Association.* https://doi.org/10.1093/jeea/jvaf016 Retrieved from https://academic.oup.com/jeea/advance-article/doi/10.1093/jeea/jvaf016/8112864 [last accessed 09 Oct 2025]

5 Pettinger, T. (2025). *Are young men falling behind? Economics Help.* Retrieved from https://www.economicshelp.org/blog/217578/economics/are-young-men-falling-behind/ [last accessed 09 Oct 2025]

6 Cox, D. (2021). *Men's Social Circles are Shrinking.* American Survey Center. Retrieved from https://www.americansurveycenter.org/why-mens-social-circles-are-shrinking/ [last accessed 09 Oct 2025]

7 King's College London. (2024). *Nearly half of Britons say women's equality has gone far enough.* Retrieved from https://www.kcl.ac.uk/news/nearly-half-of-britons-say-womens-equality-has-gone-far-enough [last accessed 09 Oct 2025]

8 Brierley, J. (2025). *A 5-fold increase . . . The phenomenal rise in young men attending church. Dr Rhiannon McAleer on the UK's 'Quiet Revival'.* Retrieved from https://justinbrierley.beehiiv.com/p/a-5-fold-increase-the-phenomenal-rise-in-young-men-attending-church-dr-rhiannon-mcaleer-on-the-uk-s [last accessed 09 Oct 2025]

9 King's College London. (2024). *Nearly half of Britons say women's equality has gone far enough.* Retrieved from https://www.kcl.ac.uk/news/nearly-half-of-britons-say-womens-equality-has-gone-far-enough [last accessed 09 Oct 2025]

10 Graham, R. (2024). *In a First Among Christians, Young Men Are More Religious Than Young Women. The New York Times.* Retrieved from https://

www.nytimes.com/2024/09/23/us/young-men-religion-gen-z.html [last accessed 09 Oct 2025]

11 Regehr, K., Shaughnessy, C., Zhao, M., & Shaughnessy, N. (2024). *Safer scrolling: How algorithms popularise and gamify online hate and misogyny for young people* [PDF]. Association of School and College Leaders (ASCL). Retrieved from https://www.ascl.org.uk/ASCL/media/ASCL/Help%20and%20advice/Inclusion/Safer-scrolling.pdf [last accessed 09 Oct 2025]

12 Desmarais, A. (2024). *TikTok and YouTube Shorts push misogynistic videos to young male watchers, study finds. Euronews.* Retrieved from https://www.euronews.com/next/2024/04/23/tiktok-and-youtube-shorts-push-misogynistic-videos-to-young-male-watchers-study-finds [last accessed 09 Oct 2025]

13 Regehr, K., Shaughnessy, C., Zhao, M., & Shaughnessy, N. (2024). *Safer scrolling: How algorithms popularise and gamify online hate and misogyny for young people* [PDF]. Association of School and College Leaders (ASCL). Retrieved from https://www.ascl.org.uk/ASCL/media/ASCL/Help%20and%20advice/Inclusion/Safer-scrolling.pdf [last accessed 09 Oct 2025]

14 Desmarais, A. (2024). *TikTok and YouTube Shorts push misogynistic videos to young male watchers, study finds. Euronews.* Retrieved from https://www.euronews.com/next/2024/04/23/tiktok-and-youtube-shorts-push-misogynistic-videos-to-young-male-watchers-study-finds [last accessed 09 Oct 2025]

15 Imm, C. (2023, March 3). *Untilled Earth: The causes and dangers of America's single young men. Midwestern Citizen.* Retrieved from https://midwesterncitizen.substack.com/p/untilled-earth-the-causes-and-dangers [last accessed 09 Oct 2025]

16 Dyrendal, A., Kennair, L. E. O., & Bendixen, M. (2021). *Predictors of belief in conspiracy theory: The role of individual differences in schizotypal traits, paranormal beliefs, social dominance orientation, right-wing authoritarianism, and conspiracy mentality. Personality and Individual Differences, 182*, 110645. https://doi.org/10.1016/j.paid.2021.110645 Retrieved from https://www.sciencedirect.com/science/article/pii/S0191886921000209? [last accessed 09 Oct 2025]

17 Freeman, D., & Bentall, R. P. (2017). *The concomitants of conspiracy concerns. Social psychiatry and psychiatric epidemiology, 52*(5), 595–604. https://doi.org/10.1007/s00127-017-1354-4 Retrieved from https://pmc.ncbi.nlm.nih.gov/articles/PMC5423964/ [last accessed 09 Oct 2025]

18 Kobayashi, Y., & Tanaka, S. (2024). *How gender shapes attitudes and concerns about immigration. Politics, Groups, and Identities.* Advance online publication. https://doi.org/10.1080/21565503.2024.2378023 Retrieved from https://www.tandfonline.com/journals/rpgi20 [last accessed 09 Oct 2025]
19 Monroe, M., Baker, R. C., & Roll, S. (1997). *The relationship of homophobia to intimacy in heterosexual men. Journal of homosexuality, 33*(2), 23–37. https://doi.org/10.1300/J082v33n02_02 Retrieved from https://pubmed.ncbi.nlm.nih.gov/9210011/ [last accessed 09 Oct 2025]
20 Cox, D. (2021). *Men's Social Circles are Shrinking.* American Survey Center. Retrieved from https://www.americansurveycenter.org/why-mens-social-circles-are-shrinking/ [last accessed 09 Oct 2025]
21 Barchester Healthcare. (2016). *Men more likely to struggle with emotional support, study finds.* Retrieved from https://mentalhealth.barchester.com/news/men-more-likely-struggle-emotional-support [last accessed 09 Oct 2025]
22 Schmidt, A. (2025). *Why the male loneliness epidemic is really the male violence epidemic. Medusa Media Collective.* Retrieved from https://medusamediacollective.com/male-loneliness-or-violence/ [last accessed 09 Oct 2025]
23 Choudhury, N. (2022). *Research finds that 97% of women in the UK have been sexually harassed. Open Access Government.* Retrieved from https://www.openaccessgovernment.org/97-of-women-in-the-uk/105940/ [last accessed 09 Oct 2025]
24 Rape Crisis England & Wales (n.d.). *Rape and sexual assault statistics.* Retrieved from https://rapecrisis.org.uk/get-informed/statistics-sexual-violence/ [last accessed 09 Oct 2025]
25 RAINN (Rape, Abuse & Incest National Network). (n.d.). *Criminal justice system statistics.* Retrieved from https://rainn.org/statistics/criminal-justice-system [last accessed 09 Oct 2025]
26 Lawtons Solicitors. (2024). *Marital Rape Law in the UK: A 2024 Guide.* Retrieved from https://www.lawtonslaw.co.uk/resources/what-are-the-legal-penalties-for-marital-rape/ [last accessed 09 Oct 2025]
27 Parker, A. (2023). *Virtually all rape victims are denied justice: Here is the roadmap to failure. Saunders Solicitors.* Retrieved from https://www.saunders.co.uk/news/virtually-all-rape-survivors-are-denied-justice-here-is-the-roadmap-to-failure/ [last accessed 09 Oct 2025]
28 Choudhury, N. (2022). *Research finds that 97% of women in the UK have*

been sexually harassed. Open Access Government. Retrieved from https://www.openaccessgovernment.org/97-of-women-in-the-uk/105940/ [last accessed 09 Oct 2025]

29 Basile, K. C., Chen, J., Friar, N. W., Smith, S. G., & Leemis, R. W. (2024). *Association of Contact Sexual Violence Victimization and Health in the U.S. American journal of preventive medicine, 66*(5), 860–869. https://doi.org/10.1016/j.amepre.2024.01.022 Retrieved from https://pmc.ncbi.nlm.nih.gov/articles/PMC11182425/ [last accessed 09 Oct 2025]

30 RAINN (Rape, Abuse & Incest National Network). (n.d.). *Criminal justice system statistics.* Retrieved from https://rainn.org/statistics/criminal-justice-system [last accessed 09 Oct 2025]

31 Lee, G. (2018). *Men are more likely to be raped than be falsely accused of rape. Channel 4 News.* Retrieved from https://www.channel4.com/news/factcheck/factcheck-men-are-more-likely-to-be-raped-than-be-falsely-accused-of-rape [last accessed 09 Oct 2025]

32 Hohl, K. (2022, April 4). *New scorecards show under 1% of reported rapes lead to conviction – criminologist explains why England's justice system continues to fail. City, University of London.* Retrieved from https://www.citystgeorges.ac.uk/news-and-events/news/2022/04/new-scorecards-show-under-1-of-reported-rapes-lead-to-conviction-criminologist-explains-why-englands-justice-system-continues-to-fail [last accessed 09 Oct 2025]

33 Rape Crisis England & Wales (n.d.). *Rape and sexual assault statistics.* Retrieved from https://rapecrisis.org.uk/get-informed/statistics-sexual-violence/ [last accessed 09 Oct 2025]

34 National Sexual Violence Resource Center (NSVRC). (2024). *Statistics.* Retrieved from https://www.nsvrc.org/statistics [last accessed 09 Oct 2025]

35 Choudhury, N. (2022). *Research finds that 97% of women in the UK have been sexually harassed. Open Access Government.* Retrieved from https://www.openaccessgovernment.org/97-of-women-in-the-uk/105940/ [last accessed 09 Oct 2025]

36 Rape Crisis England & Wales (n.d.). *Rape and sexual assault statistics.* Retrieved from https://rapecrisis.org.uk/get-informed/statistics-sexual-violence/ [last accessed 09 Oct 2025]

37 Rape Crisis England & Wales. (2025). *Recent developments on tackling child rape and sexual abuse.* Retrieved from https://rapecrisis.org.uk/news/recent-developments-on-child-rape-and-sexual-abuse/ [last accessed 09 Oct 2025]

38 Humboldt State University. (2023). *Sexualized violence statistics.* Retrieved from https://www.humboldt.edu/supporting-survivors/educational-resources/statistics [last accessed 09 Oct 2025]

39 Parker, A. (2023). *Virtually all rape victims are denied justice: Here is the roadmap to failure. Saunders Solicitors.* Retrieved from https://www.saunders.co.uk/news/virtually-all-rape-victims-are-denied-justice-here-is-the-roadmap-to-failure/ [last accessed 09 Oct 2025]

40 Lee, G. (2018). *Men are more likely to be raped than be falsely accused of rape. Channel 4 News.* Retrieved from https://www.channel4.com/news/factcheck/factcheck-men-are-more-likely-to-be-raped-than-be-falsely-accused-of-rape [last accessed 09 Oct 2025]

41 Parker, A. (2023). *Virtually all rape victims are denied justice: Here is the roadmap to failure. Saunders Solicitors.* Retrieved from https://www.saunders.co.uk/news/virtually-all-rape-victims-are-denied-justice-here-is-the-roadmap-to-failure/ [last accessed 09 Oct 2025]

42 Adams, L. (2018). *Sex attack victims usually know attacker, says new study. BBC News.* Retrieved from https://www.bbc.co.uk/news/uk-scotland-43128350 [last accessed 09 Oct 2025]

43 Rape Crisis England & Wales. (2024). *Lifetime cost of sexual violence revealed.* Retrieved from https://rapecrisis.org.uk/news/lifetime-cost-of-sexual-violence-revealed/ [last accessed 09 Oct 2025]

44 Gollasch, G. (2025). *UK ad spend surpasses £40bn for first time. Marketing Week.* Retrieved from https://www.marketingweek.com/uk-ad-spend-growth-2024/# [last accessed 09 Oct 2025]

45 Elkin, M. (2021). *Violence against women and girls: Helping to understand the scale and impact of the problem.* Office for National Statistics (ONS). Retrieved from https://blog.ons.gov.uk/2021/11/24/violence-against-women-and-girls-helping-to-understand-the-scale-and-impact-of-the-problem/ [last accessed 09 Oct 2025]

46 Vodafone UK. (2019). *New research shows how domestic violence and abuse affects UK workplace.* Retrieved from https://www.vodafone.co.uk/newscentre/press-release/new-research-shows-how-domestic-violence-and-abuse-affects-uk-workplace/ [last accessed 09 Oct 2025]

47 Brown, S., Khasteganan, N., Brown, K., Hegarty, K., Carter, G., Tarzia, L., Feder, G., & O'Doherty, L. (2019). *Psychosocial interventions for survivors of rape and sexual assault experienced during adulthood (Protocol). Cochrane Database*

of Systematic Reviews, 2019(11), CD013456. https://doi.org/10.1002/14651858. CD013456 Retrieved from https://pure.coventry.ac.uk/ws/portalfiles/portal/27636508/Binder4.pdf [last accessed 09 Oct 2025]

CREDITS

Orion Ignite would like to thank everyone at Orion who worked on the publication of *It's a Rich Man's World.*

Agent
Oscar Janson-Smith

Editor
Anna Argenio

Copy-editor
Jenni Davis

Proofreader
Simon Fox

Editorial Management
Naomi Morris Omori
Pablo Pizarro Janczur
Jane Hughes
Charlie Panayiotou
Lucy Bilton
Patrice Nelson

Audio
Paul Stark
Louise Richardson
Georgina Cutler-Ross

Contracts
Rachel Monte
Ellie Bowker
Tabitha Gresty

Design
Tomás Almeida
Nick Shah
Deborah Francois
Helen Ewing

Finance
Nick Gibson
Jasdip Nandra
Sue Baker
Tom Costello

Inventory
Jo Jacobs
Dan Stevens

Production
Hannah Cox
Katie Horrocks

Marketing
Javerya Iqbal

Publicity
Sarah Lundy

Sales
Dave Murphy
Victoria Laws
Sammy Luton
Group Sales teams across
Digital, Field, International
and Non-Trade

Operations
Group Sales Operations team

Rights
Rebecca Folland
Tara Hiatt
Ben Fowler
Maddie Stephenson
Ruth Blakemore
Marie Henckel